the GIRL in SASKATOON

# SHARON BUTALA

## the GIRL in SASKATOON

A Meditation on Friendship, Memory, and Murder

A PHYLLIS BRUCE BOOK
HARPERCOLLINS PUBLISHERS LTD

*The Girl in Saskatoon*
© 2008 by Sharon Butala. All rights reserved.

A Phyllis Bruce Book, published by HarperCollins Publishers Ltd.

First Edition

HarperCollins books may be purchased for educational, business, or sales promotional use through our Special Markets Department.

HarperCollins Publishers Ltd
2 Bloor Street East, 20th Floor
Toronto, Ontario, Canada
M4W 1A8

*www.harpercollins.ca*

Library and Archives Canada Cataloguing in Publication

Butala, Sharon, 1940–
The girl in Saskatoon : a meditation on friendship, memory, and murder /
Sharon Butala. — 1st ed.


"A Phyllis Bruce book".

ISBN 978-0-00-200720-7


1. Wiwcharuk, Alexandra. 2. Murder—Saskatchewan—Saskatoon. 3. Murder
victims—Saskatchewan—Saskatoon—Biography. I. Title.

HV6535.C33S36 2008    364.152'309712425    C2007-907027-2


HC 9 8 7 6 5 4 3 2 1

Printed and bound in the United States

*This book is for Alex*
*and for*
*the Wiwcharuk family*

# Imminence

A girl sits at the river. She sits alone, her knees pulled up to her chin, her arms wrapped around them, in the centre of the concrete apron that spreads itself between the high, black-iron railway bridge some distance to her left, and the weir closer to her on her right over which the river pours unceasingly, dropping to boil and foam, and making a steady, not unpleasant, whispering roar as backdrop to the stillness of the warm spring evening.

Off to the girl's right, a boy casts his line into the water below the weir at the fish ladder, where an abundance of fish tumble and jump. On the girl's left, on the apron but nearer to the bridge, there is a shadowy figure. The girl—or more properly, a young woman—dark, small, and exquisitely pretty, appears lost in her thoughts, oblivious to both the fisherman and the person in the shadows, and also to the two boys who stand at the low, ineffectual rope-and-post fence above and behind, staring longingly down at her.

She sits, looking out over the river as the moon slowly rises to skim the dark water with its silver light. She might be waiting for someone, positioned as she is in a prominent spot, the more easily to be seen. A lover, a friend. Or perhaps like the rest of the city she's been made a bit dreamy by spring's arrival, and wants only to feel the soft warmth of the air a little longer before night sets in. Perhaps she is dreaming of the spring of her forest childhood, how she ran through the wet, greening pastures, the ragged, noisy Vs of geese passing overhead, how she gathered purple crocuses to take back to the cramped farmhouse for her mother. Or maybe her memories are slowly dissolved by her current dissatisfactions, the disappointing certainty, the dull rhythm of her days at the hospital where she nurses, the irritating sameness of desire among the abundance of young men in her life. Maybe she has begun to dream of a more fulfilling future: travel to exotic countries— impenetrable green jungles or vast gleaming deserts, or many-spired cities—glittering parties, brilliant, handsome men, her own place among the powerful of the world. Maybe she is thinking how she will leave this little city, go somewhere else, how she is ready to take that first, daring step from her old, tight little life into a limitless new one.

Danger is present as she sits there; surely guardian angels also hover around her; the air is fraught with imminence, and the girl sits, clasping her knees with her arms, gazing out over the river, unaware that she is about to die.

# Preface

One soft spring evening in 1962 a young nurse named Alexandra Wiwcharuk was murdered and an entire city came to a stop: Alexandra's murder was all anyone could talk about. It has been forty-four years as I write this, and her killer has never been identified. I remember this, in part, because I knew her. Although Alex's home was a farm a few miles from Endeavour, Saskatchewan, on the far east side of the province, instead of attending high school in the small city of Yorkton an hour south of her home, she was sent 125 miles west to Saskatoon to enrol in the same school I would attend. There we would meet, and from that time on, our lives would be linked.

Forty-four years later, at a social gathering in the same city, a well-known writer who had moved to Saskatoon only two years after Alex's death said to me, "Do you know that Saskatoon people have never forgotten that murder. They *all* remember it, and they *still* talk about it." I did know that, but the way he said it struck a chord deep inside me, plangent, heart-stopping, and catching me by surprise, as if this were news that I was hearing for the first time. His remark had been unprompted, and it was made with such conviction, expressing, at the same time, his surprise; his voice was even tinged with something that might have been awe. I knew that sound well, that mix of surprise, dismay, chagrin, bafflement, and wonder, but in the long years—a good ten by then—of my quest to understand Alex's murder and the city's continuing memory of it, and in my dogged gathering of myriad details, I had nearly forgotten. But he is right: it is extraordinary that her death is still remembered.

Without giving it much thought, over the years I had told people that I'd never forgotten what happened to Alex because we spent four years together in the same high school, and perhaps that is the main reason. But I am only one of hundreds of people, most of whom had never even heard of her before the night of her death, who still recall, sometimes with tears in their eyes or a touch of huskiness in their voices, exactly what they were doing when the news of her murder reached them, or how they went down to the riverbank that same night, or the next, in a kind of shocked suspension of belief, as if being at the actual site where her body was found could make her death real. As if a crowd of strangers standing together, silently staring at the place where she was said to have died, could make clear that she was indeed dead, and in the appalling manner the newspaper had reported.

*We* haven't forgotten, people would say, because she was young and beautiful, she was just beginning her life, and so her death was tragic. Others would say, though, that the real reason we can't forget is that her killer was never caught, never even guessed at with any certainty. It is because there has been no closure, people would say, plaintively, that we can't forget. Or, they would say, after all, hers was the first murder of its kind in this city, an historic marker of sorts. Or, they would insist, the reason we can't forget is that her murder was so savage, so brutal; we remember it in proportion to its horror. How could we forget?

But the more I study this inability to forget, the lack of the desire to forget—or, to put it positively, the extraordinary constancy with which Alex is remembered—the more I think there must be deeper reasons than those I have mentioned. I think those deeper reasons are to be found in an examination of who we were as a society then—Saskatoon, Saskatchewan, in 1962—and where we had all come from, and why. They are also to be found in an investigation of who Alexandra—sometimes spelled Alexandria—Wiwcharuk was, as well as any of us can tell, since she was barely twenty-three years old at her death—of what had formed her, and where she might have been going or been expected to go, had she not died. They are influenced by the way in which she, a smart, very pretty, but apparently otherwise unexceptional young woman could stand, at some level, for each of us. To try to answer these questions—who she was, where she came from—I had to study not just her life but the manner of her death, and the response to it of those in power—the police, the justice system—and not just of her grieving family and friends, but also of the ordinary people of the city who still remember and feel a never-diminishing pity for her.

I also have had to inquire into my own life. I was her contemporary, a girl formed in much the same way that she had been formed, and by social factors we then took as authentic, inalterable facts about the world. I am speaking of the fifties ambience, the fifties ethic, and the fifties world of pop culture: movies, music, books, television, the new world of advertising. We had been acquaintances, never close friends, and if at the time we knew each other we felt ourselves to be very different—she was a Ukrainian farm girl (her surname, Wiwcharuk, is pronounced something like Vee-chair-ook), while my background is a mixture of French, Scottish, and Irish, and although both my parents came from farms, I had never lived on one—we felt ourselves different only because of the cultural climate of the time and place. To this, add the fact that she grew up to be beautiful, while I did not. In fact, it would be a long time—years—before I would be able to recognize how alike we were in the ways that matter. Yet, pairing us in whatever way I might, the fact remains that I lived and have had a life, even managing to fulfill some of my high school dreams, while for Alex, everything ended that night on the riverbank in Saskatoon.

When I began to wonder, as a writer, what her true story was, I meant by that only what exactly had happened the night she was killed, who the suspects were, and why no one was ever caught. I thought, if I thought at all, that if I knew those things, it would be enough. But as the years passed and I began to find answers to those questions, the more answers I found, the more inadequate they seemed; the more I discovered, the less I felt I knew. At last I began to see that, interesting as those answers might sometimes be, they failed to satisfy me because they were the answers to the wrong questions.

After some ten years of thinking, talking to people, asking questions, and reading old newspaper reports and whatever documents I could lay my hands on, I had finally come to see that the question that had to be the trenchant one, the real one, almost the only one, encompassing as it does all the other questions from *Who did it?* to *What really happened that night?* and *Which of the many rumours about that night, about her killer or killers, are true?* to *How could such evil happen in our decent, small city?* was this: *Why this constancy of memory?* And further: *What purpose is served by it? In a world where horrific deaths on a vast scale—three thousand in a moment in New York City, thousands in Afghanistan and Iraq—in a world of suicide bombers, whose purpose, whose need, is it that we should never forget one pretty young woman's death in Saskatoon?* In the end, I began to see that the real question was less about the specifics of her murder and of the investigation, and more about why I needed so badly to know, *why* no factual answers satisfied me, why I, too, could not forget.

In that moment, at the social gathering when the writer inadvertently reminded me of how we all—strangers and friends alike—remembered, I saw where I had gone wrong, how my half-written book about Alex's life and death had failed to address the resonant world of deeper meaning, had answered the wrong questions. This is the new book, the one that tries to make her alive and real again so that—in some small way—her suffering might be redeemed.

## Chapter One
## By the River

I was sitting in my car at the city's far south end, on the high east side of the South Saskatchewan River, and gazing down and across the half-mile-or-better expanse to the west bank. It was late spring and everything was green on that sunny day, the sky blue and cloudless, the opposite bank covered in greenery and looking, in the clear but delicate spring light, as if it might be capable of simply floating away, widening the river, or drifting toward me to make it vanish entirely. And the river, silver and blue that morning, although close up, I knew it would be a brownish green and mostly opaque, and beyond that green forest on the opposite bank, far beyond, more trees, a few rooftops, and then on the other side of the long, low hill which prevented me from seeing it, there would be the prairie. In my mind's eye I saw the prairie billowing out like a shook feather quilt, in squares of green or brown or the palest cream, and dotted, here and there, with the chance embroidery of trees and shrubs.

I got out of my car and walked to the edge of the high, grassy bank, at a place where no bushes rose to block my view. Far below, the sun glistened on the deceptively placid water, especially where it lapped shallowly at the edge of a long, tan sandbar, and to the right of that bar, on another which was submerged just enough that the long-legged birds that gathered there stood in water. They were brown and grey, fat and sassy, with long curved beaks, though from that distance I couldn't actually see this, and they spread their wings easily or quarrelsomely, then settled back with self-important shakes. To their left, on the sandbar that rose a few inches above the gentle rippling of the shallow amber water, I could see a flock of birds so white that in the sunlight they appeared incandescent. I could not make out what kind they were, except that they were not the snow geese or the wild swans that might be seen at that time of year in Saskatchewan on large, isolated bodies of water. I didn't want to call them seagulls—seagulls squawk and flap and are annoying scavengers—although I suspected that they were, but for some reason the field glasses usually kept in the car were not there so I couldn't identify them.

I returned reluctantly to my car and got back into the driver's seat, still looking out across the river. Back of the green-clad banks on the other side I could pick out a few cars making their antlike ways north or west down the narrow roads, appearing and disappearing through trees, the occasional building obscuring them for a moment before they emerged again, and, watching them, and the birds far below on the water, and the way the sun made the river gleam and sparkle, made it *dance*, I was stricken with love. *How I love this city*, I thought, and was surprised enough by this that my thoughts seemed to stop, and I said again, out loud, tentatively this time, maybe closer to a question than a statement: "I *love* this city?"

I was as baffled as astonished at this revelation, because it had been the scene of some rough times in my life, the roughest times: my harsh introduction to city life had been here, I had married and divorced here, I had once had a career here and in sheer disgust and something close to despair, and against the helpless protests of others, I had turned my back on it. Not that I thought specifically of all those things at that moment, but I did think that I had as much reason to hate this city as to love it, and now I wondered why I hadn't thought, just as spontaneously, *I hate this place.*

I thought, but of course I love it right now, because this morning in this wonderful spring light, and at this point high above it, this city is so beautiful, as beautiful as a landscape in a dream or a children's book of stories. But, I argued with myself, you weren't born here; you didn't even live here for more than—what?—about seventeen years all told. Isn't home the place where you were born, where you were an infant and a child? For me, that would be the east central part of the province on the very edge of the boreal forest. And, thirty years earlier, I had married a rancher and for years have lived in the far southwest of the province. Surely I had relinquished any right to call anywhere else but the southwest home; surely I should have no need; surely I could not really desire to do so. And yet, carried away for a moment by the city's beauty, and also by my strong sense of familiarity, so intense that it did not involve reason, I *had* called this city home; I had admitted it is home in my soul. But instead of satisfying me, this insight made me uneasy, as if I were missing something, something important about my own life.

The river below me, the South Saskatchewan, bisects the city at about an eighty-degree angle from southwest to northeast as it flows from the western Rockies on to join the North Saskatchewan west of the small city of Prince Albert, called for as long as I can remember "The Gateway to the North." The river flows past the village where I started school, then where we lived for a couple of (in my memory) desolate years before I was school age, runs a few miles south of the homestead where I spent the earliest years of my life, and then on northeast past the place where I was born, also north of the area where Alex was born and lived the first fifteen years of her life, before it loses itself in the busy, complicated, and magnificently wild network of rivers and lakes in northern Saskatchewan and Manitoba. Eventually it empties into Hudson Bay, where, as every schoolchild learns, Henry Hudson tried to find the famed North-West Passage in 1611 and was set adrift on the open sea by his mutinous crew.

The river has always defined the city, been the highway for the First Nations peoples and a rich source of food, and one of great hope—unfulfilled—for the earliest settlers. Eventually, today, dammed and no longer so wild, it makes beautiful what otherwise might have been a neatly boring plains city. Only a few parts of its riverbank, all downtown, were parks when Alex and I were in high school, but today all of its banks within the city limits are protected and managed, and most of it is parkland, and in good weather these parks are full of people strolling, picnicking, playing Frisbee, romping with dogs, and toddlers. That river *is* Saskatoon, as it was when we were young, and despite the new suburbs with their own busy lives, swimming pools, strip malls, tennis courts, churches, that have sprung up far from its banks.

I started the car and drove on slowly farther south, down the road to Diefenbaker Park, where the road ended and where I would have to turn around. But first I drove into the park and stopped on one of the small asphalt-covered areas designed as lookout points, so that I could stare out, once more, across the river. I was flooded by memories then. For instance, I remembered (or thought I did) when in January of every year the city used to collect all the discarded Christmas trees and have a huge bonfire here. That would have been in the late sixties or early seventies. What had once been a huge, empty area without a tree when the city had finally gone seriously to work on making this piece of land into Diefenbaker Park (after originally obtaining it around 1930 by default of unpaid taxes, and then doing virtually nothing with it into the sixties) was now beautifully landscaped and carefully tended. Times had changed. The idea of having a twenty- or fifty-foot blaze in the park's centre now was clearly absurd, if not downright offensive.

The memory or pseudo-memory of the fiery pyre surrounded by city-dwellers and their children, all bundled in heavy parkas and ski pants, standing in the darkness of a frigid winter evening, the firelight flickering on their upturned faces and their clothing, casting gold and red light, faded slowly. I turned back to the wide, clear view. I missed seeing through the buoyant, blue-green surface of the trees across the river, the bright accents of the red tile roofs of the old tuberculosis sanatarium and doctor's residence that had once been there. My mother had worked nights for a brief time around 1953 as the guardian—my tiny, sweet, dauntingly intelligent mother—in the nurses' residence. And she had once caught a couple of young nurses, well after midnight, sneaking in through an open window. I remember overhearing her as she told my father about it, but to my surprise, as she would have *killed* any one of us, her daughters, for such a crime, she didn't seem upset over it.

I widened my gaze to where the new—fairly new, commissioned about 1959—Queen Elizabeth power plant, a large building, red-brown brick on the bottom, silver-white on the top half, with its three tall chimneys, sat dominating the view to my left. It sat even beyond the CNR bridge, at the far south end of the road called Spadina Crescent that ran north and south through the heart of the city, all the way to the river's west edge. Sometimes, on a sunny weekend in the warm months, we kids biked or walked to the road's end where eventually the power plant would be built and while the sanatarium was still there. I don't know if the place held such an attraction for us because we were children and children especially crave trees and grass and the proximity of natural bodies of water—children being closer to creation than adults—or because most of us had spent our earliest, most impressionable years on farms or homesteads in the wilderness and were drawn to such a place as one is drawn to whatever one knows first, as the right place, the true place. Of all my childhood memories of this city, going with my friends along that dirt road lined with trees and shrubs, the river flowing beside us, is one that clings to me.

I remembered, too, that this was the place where the frozen bodies of two Aboriginal men were found in January and Feb-ruary, 2000. (Two others were found elsewhere, one of them back in 1990.) How these men came to be there, not even properly dressed for outdoors in a prairie winter, remains a mystery, one fraught with undertones of—well—evil. The rest of the city lay behind me, or to my right, and it was hard to see because of the thick planting of trees, but far off to my right, I thought I could see the tower of Westmount Elementary School on its hill rising above the surrounding houses. *Imagine that*, I thought, for all the other really old schools, for one rea-son or another had been torn down, and for one second I was again transported back to my elementary school days.

I turned away then, went back to my car, and drove back toward the city centre. I'd decided to cross the river to the city's west half, to drive north the length of Spadina Crescent, which meant the length of the river, just to see, if I could, the ways in which all of it had changed since I was a child. Or maybe I had no idea of that; maybe I wanted to think about this strange notion of loving this place, and to experience that while I passed through the parts of the city I knew best.

Once across the river, I turned north, and joining Spadina Crescent at the heart of downtown, just past the beautiful old railway hotel, the Bessborough, I began to drive slowly along the river, past the cathedrals on my left and eventually past the row of stately homes that face the river, some of which had been built a hundred years earlier by the first city fathers. Finally I arrived at the weir, and just beyond it, the CPR bridge that since 1908 has crossed the river there, and also Spadina Crescent, so that I would have to drive under it. From there, the railway continues through the city by running onto the built-up embankment parallel to 33rd Street. Since the earliest part of the twentieth century the heart of Saskatoon has been bounded by the two railway bridges. I had just driven from the far south end, where the CNR bridge still stands, and that still marks that farther edge of the city, to the CPR bridge that had once marked the north boundary; nowadays the city has spread well past it.

At the point where the bridge passes overhead, Spadina Crescent is narrow and the houses that face the river, although nicely kept, are hardly mansions. The landscape is grassy, dotted with shrubs and sometimes trees, or covered with asphalt, bits of gravel scattered along the street's edges. I had been thinking, *But how could anyone tell?* From my low vantage point as I drove slowly past, the place appeared as mundane, as unprepossessing as any in the city. It was nothing, it seemed to me then, it was nowhere, and I faltered and was puzzled, because without realizing it, I had wanted this spot to be resting under a permanent cloud of dark memory, something that as you approached would settle on you, seep into your bones, into your very soul, so that you could not help but know that something had happened here.

This was where Alex was last seen alive; this was also where she had died. I had an urge to stop, to park, but I had done that many times over the past few years, and I was struggling with emotion that I could not understand: How could things so terrible happen without there being any way to tell? How could such emotion be spilled here and leave no trace? Years after Alex's death I had been in Iraklion on Crete and at the grave of Nikos Kazantzakis had broken into sobs that I could neither stop nor understand, except as an artifact of the hundreds who had sobbed there at his burial, a flow of emotion so powerful that it still hung there—and so I knew such things could happen. I thought that they should, and to everyone, to greater or lesser degree, whenever we stand at places on the earth where terrible things once happened. But I saw nothing out of the ordinary, and so I drove on slowly, thinking about this as I went, north on Spadina Crescent along the river, until the street name changed to Whiteswan Drive where I passed the large new houses, with their mostly derivative architecture (Cape Cod, Tudor, weathered Atlantic cottage, southern American plantation).

The fact that there was no way to tell that a young, innocent, and beautiful woman had been violated, beaten, and killed next to the CPR bridge shocked and dismayed me; I did not want anyone ever to forget what had happened there so many years before. That people could come as strangers to the city now, and never know, not even want to know, hurt me—and almost immediately, frightened me. I felt a sudden, gut-wrenching fear, because if we didn't remember, had no reminders at all of such a tragic event, then such a thing might happen to any of us, and the failure to remember would relegate it to the realm of the commonplace, the absolvable, the unnoteworthy. Not that when I felt that spasm of fear I understood it at once; only in later ruminations did I begin to see.

I noticed then that the two spots I'd made a point of visiting, and that had evoked in me a visceral sense of my relationship to the city, were also two of the places where the very worst had happened: not slums, not derelict buildings, not prisons or hospitals for the insane, or environmentally destroyed sites, but the places wherein the city's infamy also lay. The very places where the beauty was greatest, where for several generations (although the city was only one hundred years old in 2006) Saskatoon people have gone to enjoy themselves on a Sunday afternoon or a warm summer evening or to toboggan in the winter, were also the places where terrible things happened, sometimes where unspeakable deeds were done: beautiful as they were, these were the places, also, where evil had triumphed. This is what I was thinking as I drove slowly on down Whiteswan Drive, the river flowing with me on my right, and the row of large, gracious houses on my left, appearing, looming, and retreating as I passed.

Well into my sixties as I write this, I was—I am—at last, in the process of facing the existence of evil, of trying to formulate some understanding of it that makes sense to me, never mind anybody else, and that, at the same time, will allow me to live. It seemed to me then that those locations in the heart of the city I'd only just discovered I loved, those that were so beautiful that day, or were usually so beautiful, acted as a metaphor for how I was beginning to understand life. Evil exists everywhere at every minute, just as good does, or the potential for both. And each of us is both subject to and object of both. Worse, in the constant, unending battle of good and evil, evil wins far too often, maybe even more often than good does. That is how I am beginning to understand life.

I couldn't help but wonder how I could get so old without recognizing something so basic, how it could be that at such an age I had still failed to even try to conceptualize evil as anything other than the fire-and-brimstone hell of my forties Catholic upbringing. Over the years and without my noticing, evil had somehow become equated with rule-breaking or convention-breaking, rather than evil as measured by the harm done in the world. *Such wilful innocence*, I raged at myself, *such*—I wanted to say, *such evil innocence*—but I stopped myself. Refusing to see the truth that is all around you is not innocence; it is not the same as being unacquainted with the fact of the evil all around us.

But earlier that morning, as I'd been idly driving around the city and, for no good reason I could identify, finding myself passing the house that had been my mother's—*I loved my house,* she told us on her deathbed—noting an old building in the process of being torn down, a building in which one of my sisters had once worked, choosing to drive by a church that had been turned into a theatre, and then, to my own bemusement, the house where at a party when I was only nineteen and newly dumped by the first man I'd ever genuinely loved, I had fallen under the spell of the man who became my first husband, I hadn't been thinking about evil. I hadn't been thinking about what happened to Alex, or about the book I was trying to write about her murder. I was thinking only about how we had once lived our lives between those two bridges, within sight and sound of the constantly flowing, constantly changing river, as it wound its way through the heart of the old city where both Alex and I once were young.

It seemed to me that despite the conversions or destructions, big or small, the new buildings and the modernizing, this central part of the city had kept its essential character. I was beginning to see the city as a living, breathing entity that could not, at its deepest level, be truly changed, its character expressing itself in an ambience that, no matter how many buildings were torn down and new ones built, could never be fully altered or eradicated. It was something in the air, a kind of muggy, invisible soul that touched everything. I was thinking how Alex, transported back from the unknown place to which she was so ruthlessly and too early sent, would still know where she was; she would still recognize it.

❋

I had come to the city to attend a book launch and reception. This had happened the evening before and although it was still the first week in May, it was unbearably hot—at one point into the thirties Celsius—and at the packed reception we'd been fanning ourselves and hanging our light jackets or sweaters over our chair backs. Of course, we all attributed the unseasonable heat to global warming, the notion that weather might just be weather, having been, by then, lost forever. And so it was very hot, too hot, and we hoped that it would cool again soon because we were a little frightened by the notion of the intense heat we didn't usually have until July, now beginning the first week of May, and with the possibility of it lasting right through until fall. If it did, we would be forced to change a great deal about how we lived. Besides, the farmers' crops would be ruined by such heat and dryness, and then what? Not that any of us were farmers (except for me, and my husband was mostly a cattle rancher anyway).

It is just that in Saskatchewan, even the coolest of the city's hipsters would have to pay homage to the farmers, if with a strong sense of irony—a hint of it in the way the mouth was held, or in the slight movement of the eyebrows. In a province whose entire mythology is the mythology of land, the twenty-first century has seen radical changes, with the small farmers forced out and replaced by giant farms and agribusiness, or else by the urban well-off who turn farmland into acreages. Displaced rural and small-town people are swelling our cities. People are now taking farmers, and the farm mythology, less seriously than they used to.

The day Alex was killed, May 18, 1962 (ten days further into May than the day I have been writing about), had been very hot too, the hottest day since the previous summer, about thirty degrees Celsius. Back in 1962 we would have been merely grateful for such a beautiful day, knowing it wouldn't last, and feeling that such gorgeous weather was a gift straight from the heavens and not to be questioned. We wouldn't have been worrying about global warming or UV rays, although our parents would certainly have given a thought to what the heat would do to the farmers' crops. I don't remember the day, or what I'd been doing, although I can make a good guess because I have always been (and I say this ruefully and not without anger) helplessly predictable and dutiful.

The whole city would have been giddy with the weather, not least because of our harsh winters and the great mountains of snow we had. Everybody would have been outside to enjoy the day in the afternoon. Teenage girls would have worn as little as possible (though considerably more than they would today), shorts, I think, and sleeveless cotton blouses, because the ubiquitous "T-shirt," although around since the First World War, hadn't yet blossomed into the all-purpose, unisex garment it was to become. By evening, entire families would have been sitting on the front or back lawn, or strolling easily through the neighbourhood, radiating contentment and smiling at everyone they saw.

Of course, the boys would have been out too, usually in cars, circling neighbourhoods or heading straight downtown to cruise up and down 2nd Avenue, its main street—the one that today is mostly a parking mall—where girls would be strolling in freshly polished white sandals, cotton blouses and long, full cotton skirts, or pedal-pushers (also called capri pants), waists defined by wide, colourful, elastic cinch belts. They'd changed from shorts because appearing downtown in them was considered improper, and, if you were over ten, in bad taste. St. Paul's Hospital, on the far west side of the city, was also a training hospital and had a nurses' residence, but since I was never near there after leaving elementary school, I can only guess that boys might have cruised there too. (This was the hospital where, in 1947, one of my sisters had spent seven months being rehabilitated from a bout with polio that almost killed her, and that would, from then on, define her too-short life.) Or maybe the presence of the nuns who ran the hospital and the over-vigilant, although for the most part kindly, priests at nearby St. Mary's Church would have acted as a deterrent. Across the river, the nurses' residence at the University Hospital was inside the university grounds, and the residence too close to the hospital doors to make cruising viable.

So mostly, they would have cruised east or west down Queen Street past City Hospital. This hospital, as well as its nurses' residence, was set on the border of a large, well-groomed, and inviting park with a stream that ran through its width until it reached the edge, where it poured under Spadina Crescent and from there into the nearby river. The river and the beautiful park surrounding the hospital and residence invited strolls by people of all ages and walks of life, from dog-walkers to creaky senior citizens, to children on tricycles with their pregnant mothers, to young women, often graduate nurses or nurses in training, in pairs and groups, giggling and chattering while they kept out a weather eye for young males, and were ready to flirt at the drop of the proverbial hat.

After the boys cruised past City Hospital once, they might have turned north along Spadina Crescent heading toward the weir and the CPR bridge and, where 33rd Street meets Spadina Crescent, they'd have driven under the bridge and immediately turned west a few blocks to the corner of 7th Avenue where Mead's Drugstore was, and there turned back south along 7th Avenue, which led, once again, to the front doors of the old (1909) red-brick City Hospital with the red-brick nurses' residence between it and the river. It was a rectangular route that on beautiful spring and summer evenings practically guaranteed finding some girls to cruise along beside and try to converse with, or to entice into the car for a spin around the city.

Accepting such an invitation was an ordinary thing to do on a warm spring evening in the city then. Although our parents would have been horrified if they'd known, and we would have taken some care in deciding whether to get into the car—usually you did so only if you knew at least one of the boys or if you had a friend with you—trusting our instincts, we sometimes hopped in anyway. One of my girlfriends, who trained at City Hospital and would have been working there that spring day in 1962 when Alex vanished, met the man who became her husband in that way. She was hardly the only one. The city was a safe place, and no one I ever heard of came to harm from doing it, although I do remember once in the early fifties, standing at the bus stop at the corner of 2nd Avenue and 19th Street late one Saturday afternoon, when a car full of young people came careening by, and screeched to a stop. A girl was shoved out onto the street. The car sped away again down 19th Street, toward the underpass that used to be there and that led to the city's west side.

I remember that she staggered, but managed not to fall. She was a pretty blonde, a bit on the plump side, she carried a small white purse, and she was wearing a summer dress with a full skirt, I recall a blue and green print on a white background, an outfit that said she'd been expecting to do something special. The few of us at the bus stop, strangers to one another, pretended not to notice what had happened to her, and she stood there, holding her purse in both hands, trying not to cry, and when the bus came, she got on it with the rest of us, as if that had been her plan all along.

And now I know, of course, that if any girl who'd taken a ride in that way had been driven out into the countryside or down a dark street and raped, we would never have heard about it; it would have been kept secret, such a terrible shame it was in those days because it had to have been your fault and, in any case, recourse was virtually zero. It was better kept secret, and if you got pregnant, you'd be sent away to have the baby in secrecy and to give it away.

Alex was nursing at City Hospital in 1962, had been since late September of the year before, and that night she had to be at work for the 11:30 p.m. shift, although nowhere is it recorded on what ward. She had just turned twenty-three the month before, and it was the May long weekend, Victoria Day (which Canadians still celebrate, although I doubt there is anybody left who was alive during Queen Victoria's reign, and not many more who actually care, yet we all love the holiday). Lucky people who owned cottages at the nearby lakes—Jackfish or Emma or Christopher, or farther north at Waskesiu—would be packing their cars that night in order to head out first thing Saturday morning to open them for the summer. City kids might be driving out to Pike Lake, a half-hour to the southwest, to go for a swim, or else, car-less, wishing they could. Alex was unhappy about having to work; she'd wanted to go to her sister's cottage at either Emma Lake or Waskesiu, and had probably tried to trade shifts with somebody, but of course, everybody wanted to be off that weekend, and she'd had no takers.

She'd been on the graveyard shift the night before too, and had spent most of the afternoon of this gorgeous day sound asleep in the basement suite (as we called apartments then) that she shared with three other nurses, young women with whom she'd attended nursing school in Yorkton. Now, awake, having shared a light supper with a roommate, Alice, and a neighbour, having washed her hair and set it, then having sat under the dryer, during which time she'd written a couple of letters, one to a friend in Edmonton and one to a sister in Ontario, she changed her clothes and went out to mail the letters. That errand done, and probably not wanting to return home until it was time to go to work, she'd crossed 33rd Street at Mead's Drugstore on the corner of 7th Avenue and 33rd, only a half-block from where she lived at 1223–7th Avenue North, and walked down 33rd—not on the sidewalk, but along the grassy verge against the railway embankment, east toward Spadina Crescent and the river.

It was only a few minutes' walk, ten to fifteen at the most, although because she'd stopped to chat with someone it had taken her longer. Having arrived at the river, she turned to her right, walked under the CPR bridge, crossed Spadina Crescent to the riverbank, then the narrow, sandy parking area, stepped over the low rope-and-post fence, walked down onto the centre of the concrete apron next to the weir, and sat down, bringing her knees up to her chin and hugging them with both arms.

That was the last anyone saw of her alive. Except, of course, for her killer.

Now, as I drove past the area where she'd been killed and where nearly two weeks later her body was found, I felt a prickling unease, a fear that had transmuted into a diffuse anger that at the place where she had been murdered there was no trace left of what had happened. I was reminded how, in central Paris, there are engraved brass plaques on buildings telling everyone that at that spot in 1944, for example, two resistance fighters were shot by the Nazis. Although that plaque is there to remind people of the heroism of those men, it is also a reminder of evil, that it is always present, and that all of us need to be ever-vigilant against it. But in our civilized civic-mindedness, we don't like to be reminded of the bad things that happen, of their randomness, because we don't want to frighten children or have people develop a distaste for such a charming spot, because we don't wish to be reminded of our failures, or of the sobering, constant presence of evil.

But in that lovely, greening place that night in May 1962, with the soft whisper of the river running by, and the moonlight glistening on the water, youth, innocence, and beauty, in the person of one small Ukrainian-Canadian girl, had been stamped out. Evil had done it—pure evil—and it seemed to me then that it would continue to win, as long as Alex's killer remained unidentified and unpunished.

## Chapter Two
## Endeavour

L ooking back now, more than ten years after my
thoughts first turned to what had happened to
Alex, I think my connection to her may have
begun long before I realized it. In 1986 I had a strange dream. I
found myself in a building I recognized at once as the Ukrainian
Hall on the west side of Saskatoon, the "west side" being the west
side of the river. I once knew it well; I spent a year there attending St. Mary's School on Avenue O, and lived my life within its
boundaries and also within Riversdale, a sub-neighbourhood of
the west side, one of the oldest in the city, with its row after row of
neat, two or single-storey, small, often already worn frame houses
set close together on thirty-foot lots, with tidily trimmed cara-
gana or lilac hedges out front or low picket fences with securely
latched small gates. In those days, 1953 to 1954, all my friends
lived in those houses on Avenue G or Avenue Q or on 19th or
18th or even 23rd Street, all of which ran perpendicular to those
avenues.

In the dream, the Ukrainian Hall had become a museum,

and just in front of me, down three wide steps from the entrance area, stood a polished, pale-oak, waist-high display pedestal with an object lying on it, and a clear glass dome placed over the object. Any other display cases or furniture that might have been there, even the walls of the hall and the entrance behind me, were dissolved in shadow. There was only silence, the golden, narrow-boarded hardwood floor, and the pedestal below me. I went slowly down the steps, and I saw that the object under the glass was my journal. It was a particular journal, as I now have more than twenty-five years of them, a thick but small one whose thin paper is narrowly lined, its cover red silk with little pagodas, deer, trees, and flowers embroidered in blue and gold. It was a journal which I still think of as the heart of my journal-keeping, the one in which I recorded in the smallest detail, and on both sides of every page, the year of my deepest attempts to make my way into whole life.

There are also quotations from the many thinkers I was reading in my search for explanations of life, for guidelines as to how to be a person: Carl Jung, William James, Evelyn Underhill, Simone Weil, Thomas Merton, D. T. Suzuki, Robert Graves, Erich Neumann (from whom I learned that wood—a wooden vessel, a wooden room—is a symbol of the Great Mother). I suppose it could be said that that journal is a book about my search for soul.

When I woke, I was struck as much by the way I knew at once where I was as by the strange contents of my dream. It was clear in the dream that I had entered the Ukrainian Hall, the one that still exists on the west side on Avenue G South, between 20th and 21st streets, even though I've never actually been in it. I was surprised, too, to have found myself in my old neighbourhood, which I no longer thought of, and where I hadn't been except accidentally, driving through it on my way to somewhere else, for something like fifty years. And yet so deeply familiar to me was it that I felt as though I had some-how dreamed my way back to a place I didn't even know was home.

Trying to understand the dream, I focused on two things: first, that it was my journal under the glass case in the museum, which seemed to suggest that there was something very spe-cial about it, that it might be telling me that my books would be remembered. But I felt no particular surge of pleasure at that. In my experience, prophetic dreams tend more often to be about unforeseen disaster, not unforeseen success. The sec-ond was the Ukrainian element: I'd never been in that hall, I'm not Ukrainian, and I have never been a part of Ukrainian immigrant life in any way. And I couldn't see any connec-tion between the two ideas: my writing and Ukrainian life. I knew little, even, about Ukraine, with its very long, tumultu-ous, and complicated history, and nothing about the language. Of course, I knew—we all knew, because in Saskatchewan we all went through school with Ukrainian-speaking kids—two or three words in Ukrainian which meant "shut up," and "go away"—schoolyard rudeness in a more innocent time.

In the end, despite the dream's power, I simply stopped think-ing about it. But it had served to remind me of those early days when we first arrived in Saskatoon, a country family without urban experience and no good sense about how to live in the city, about safety, or day-to-day practices that the urban don't even think about but just do—or don't do—and how during that first year on the west side, where the city's working class people lived, the immigrants, and a small contingent of the criminal element, I lived in a state of amazement and fear, as if I had just been born and was seeing the world for the first time.

But soon after, the dream made me recall interesting events from that time: the huge excitement of the ice on the South Saskatchewan River going out in the spring, which the whole city rushed out to watch and made bets on and that some years nearly took out this bridge or that bridge; the east–west elementary school hockey game that packed the civic arena with kids from both sides of the river one fateful Satur-day morning each year, and that Roy Romanow, then a "boy broadcaster," before too long to be our premier, used to call for the radio; my crushes on boys and my first date at the old Roxy Theatre when I was fourteen, and my girlfriends, more important to me at a certain age than God or my mother or my sisters. The memories began to tumble out, vivid and emotion-laden, and filled too with a kind of wonderment at how I once lived, who I once was. Almost at once I remem-bered that among the significant or shocking things that had happened during that period, 1953 to 1962, was the murder of Alex Wiwcharuk.

I thought vaguely that maybe I could use it in a novel I was planning. But it was so odd, so out of the normal flow of things. Still, my memory had been stirred, and I thought, *But they never caught the killer, did they?* I was not even sure of that elementary fact because a year after Alex's murder, I'd left the city and the province and stayed away for five years. I was curious enough that, one day when I was in the city on other business, I stopped at the public library and searched out the microfilmed copies of the *Star Phoenix*.

I found lots of interesting facts, including that another girl Alex and I had been in high school with, many years later had been charged with being a "madam." I'd run into her in the eighties and when I expressed dismay at hearing what she was doing—she was perfectly blithe in telling me about it—she retorted angrily that it wasn't illegal (I think she meant something about the way in which she went about it), and that a certain policeman from the United States had set her up in business, or had shown her how to run such a business, which I had immediately thought was a lie, if an inspired one. But, when the newspaper did not mention that she had been fined, or sent to jail, when I realized that as nearly as I could tell she'd suffered no punishment, I couldn't help but wonder if maybe the police officer story was true.

It was a good story, all of it, and it could be made to work in my novel. And what happened to Alex would have to be worked in somehow as just one item, one incident, in what would be a long book thickly interwoven with all the stories I could remember from those days. I suppose that it would have been a kind of coming-of-age novel, but disguised—I hoped—so that it wouldn't be taken as a record of my own girlhood.

I had found a reprisal of Alex's story published in the eighties. The details were as I remembered them, but I had forgotten the specific dates, and a few other aspects such as where her poor, battered body had been found, and a little about its condition. The fact I was most interested in was reported too: that more than twenty years after her death, nobody had been accused of her murder, nor caught, nor tried, nor sent to prison. *I wonder why*, I asked myself, staring at the microfilm on the screen and feeling, for the first time, a sense of unease. Once somebody is caught and put in prison, people lose interest, but if no one is ever caught—well, that is a different story. Forgetting is harder; forgetting is near to impossible. But I didn't know that yet.

Another year or two passed, during which time, although occasionally I thought about that novel I might write, I was immersed in other projects. But then I spent much of the winter of 1997 in Saskatoon looking after a dying sister. One evening, my friends from years before, when I was still living in Saskatoon, invited me to a women's dinner, and although I had never before met some of the women there, I was seated beside one I had known since she arrived from central Canada in the early seventies. During our conversation—What was I up to? What was she up to?—I mentioned to her (and it was the first time I'd said it out loud) that I was thinking of tackling a novel about growing up in Saskatoon during the fifties and early sixties. I added, probably more in an effort to sound interesting than anything, that one of my high school girlfriends had been murdered. She said, "You mean Alexandra Wiwcharuk?"

When I got over my surprise that she would even have heard about this, she went on to say that she knew a retired policeman who had been, in some small way, involved in the original investigation and was "as obsessed with it as you are." She told me, "I can give you his name and phone number. You really must talk to him."

I was barely interested. And I was surprised, too, to hear that someone else, someone who'd actually been involved at the time, was "obsessed." I didn't think I'd ever call him and so I thanked her, not taking his name or phone number, telling her that I wasn't yet ready for that, and doubting, privately, that I ever would be. I did not, for one second, remember the strange dream about the Ukrainian Hall-Museum and the red journal under the glass dome.

After that, whenever I mentioned this book idea I had, and the fact that a girl I had known during high school had been murdered, I was careful to explain that she had never been a close friend of mine, that we'd never been in the same class, that she was only an acquaintance among many. We had been in contact with each other for four years, and then, to the best of my memory, after graduation night we never again saw each other. After some thought, though, I remembered that we'd been in drama club together for two years, although I don't think we ever acted in the same one-act play, one-acts being all we ever did in those days. Then I recalled that we'd also both been in choir, with maybe another thirty or forty kids. I could remember her clearly, her dark colouring, the neat and unassuming way she dressed—nothing flamboyant, nothing out of the ordinary—and a kind of stillness about her, which might only have been a result of the times and places where I would have seen her—at school, in group practices, when keeping quiet and paying attention was mandatory.

But I didn't remember her voice, her laughter, who her friends were, if she dated or whom, whether she was a good student or a poor one. In grade eleven and grade twelve (as with all high schools) there had been a group of girls who were the social elite, whether they were class presidents or on the students' representative council or athletes, or all three, or not. It has always been a mystery to me how these people single themselves out for such positions; I still don't know exactly what the ingredients are: they weren't necessarily the prettiest girls, or the best-dressed, or the smartest, or the best athletes—and richest wasn't even a category in our school. In any case, Alex wasn't one of that group (nor was I), and she wasn't a school leader of any kind.

As to precisely where Alex had come from, I knew only that it was a farm, but not where the farm had been. The newspaper reports said that at the time of Alex's death, her parents lived outside the city to the south, and I assumed that that must be her home, but I was uncertain, because I thought of her as someone deeply immersed in the world of Ukrainians and south of Saskatoon was not one of the places in our province where Ukrainians had settled in large numbers. Or maybe I remembered something from high school about where she had come from and I knew, in the back of my mind, that it wasn't near Saskatoon.

I can't recall when I decided to become serious about writing that book. I remember only that I felt nagged, that I couldn't seem to lose my interest; it didn't wear away as I'd expected it would. I'd finished my other projects and I was ready to begin something new. One day, I phoned the woman who had told me that she knew a retired police officer I should talk to, and asked her for his name and number. And then I wrote him a letter asking if he would be interested in meeting with me to talk about the unsolved murder of Alexandra Wiwcharuk. I was a bit nervous at my own daring, but almost at once, and to my surprise, he phoned me, pleased at my interest, and we set up a date when I would be in Saskatoon to meet for coffee. I had made no decision about a book; I was still holding off on that, waiting for something, although I wasn't sure what, but waiting for the *story*, the real one, to come into view.

As the date of our meeting drew closer, I phoned a couple of friends from our high school days, to ask them what they remembered about Alex. Nearly everyone said that he or she remembered her clearly, but there were no anecdotes, no vignettes, no conversations with her that they could tell me about. I e-mailed my sisters and they responded with stories from that time, gossip and rumours about who was responsible and why whoever it was that had killed Alex hadn't been charged, and with other stories about scandals of the same or a later era: the discovery of a brothel, in one of the city's best districts, run by a lawyer (who eventually went to jail for the crime), a former city police officer caught in a major drug-smuggling scandal in

another province (also ending up in jail), stories about a bootlegger and a bookie—who seem not to have been charged with
their crimes—and other stories I'd once known but had forgotten, stories that seemed to me, at least then, to smack more of
the incompetent and foolish than of real evil.

But nothing about Alex and that night.

One friend did remember the name of the town Alex's family
farm had been closest to: Endeavour, Saskatchewan. I looked it
up. Endeavour was not far as the crow flies from where I had
come from in east-central Saskatchewan. The north—that area
nearly empty of roads and villages (although not necessarily of
people) and covered with forest broken only by dozens of lakes,
rivers, and streams—begins in Saskatchewan above the fifty-
third line of latitude, but on the east side of the province this
area extends a long, wide finger southward a hundred miles or
so and in about a sixty-mile-wide swath. That area, too, is known
for its forests, lakes, bogs, and swamps, its plagues of mosquitoes,
and black and deer flies. The Wiwcharuk family farm, a little
north of the fifty-second line of latitude, was set on the Swan
River Plain, bordered on the north by the Pasquia Hills and to
the east by the Porcupine Hills, both of which are beautiful but
in agricultural terms impossible. North of the farm Alex was
raised on, there are only three major east-west roads and a mere
scattering of people living in villages and towns along them.

My original home, the place where I first saw life, about

two hours north and an hour and a half west of the Wiwcharuk farm, was just north of the fifty-third line of latitude.
But set a person from the Endeavour area, blindfolded, down
in Garrick (north of which my family homesteaded, and in the
forties about the same size as Endeavour, and named, astonish-
ingly, after the eighteenth-century English actor, playwright,
and director David Garrick), that person would not know the
difference. We had childhoods in wilderness, and more than
forty years after the Wiwcharuk farm was sold out of the family, and sixty after my family left, the areas are still wild.

The town of Endeavour itself, originally called Annette
after the first settler in the small community nearest to the
Wiwcharuk home, was later named after the monoplane, the
Endeavour, flown by Captain Walter Hinchcliffe in 1928 in a
bid to be the first to cross the Atlantic from east to west. The
attempt ended in a crash, killing him and his female co-pilot.
That was the same year the CNR line came through the area,
and it changed the name to Endeavour. (A nearby siding originally called Etomami, now extinct, was named Hinchcliffe
after the Endeavour's pilot. "Etomami," according to Bill Barry
in his *People Places*, is a version of the Cree *ayitaw-mâmihk*,
meaning "downstream on both sides" or "watershed." This
was a portage between the north and south Etomami River,
the south branch of which runs along the eastern border of
Endeavour and is now called the Lilian River.

Many Saskatchewan communities were named after someone or someplace far from the new community, and having
little or no relationship to the new village or hamlet that sprang

up in response to the needs of settlers and of the CNR. Actually, renamed would be a more accurate description since all such places had names in Indian languages of those who had known them for centuries, but nobody took the time to find out what those names might be, or they could not pronounce or spell the native names, or felt such "primitive" naming to be meaningless. (Sometimes the towns were given names that encapsulated the settlers' dreams—Plenty, Success, Conquest, Climax—which, before long, became ironic.) In fact, the nearest Reserve to the town is the Key (Chief Ow-tah-pee-ka-kaw) Reserve inhabited by mixed Cree and Saulteaux peoples, created in 1875 under Treaty Four. Perhaps what the settlers really felt was that by renaming a place, they were altering it forever from the wilderness abode of "savages."

So, our first experience of life—Alex's from April 1939, and mine from August 1940—was not of a neat frame, brick, or stone farmhouse in the midst of cleared and seeded fields of wheat, oats, barley, or rye, and of, within walking distance, other long-settled farms just like ours, with a pleasant, prosperous village with freshly painted white church and brick schoolhouse just over the next hill. Our first memories were of uncut, uncleared, and untamed forest, and all the worries and fears that the forest induced: fear of wolves, which we heard howling every day at sundown; of bears, of which we saw traces every day, and often caught glimpses and heard stories; fear of being lost in the endlessly wide, deep, and unbounded forest, and never found; fear, also, of who-knew-what other mysterious and dark forces, out of the realm of fairy tales.

And then there were the always-present Aboriginal peoples, pushed to the periphery of our society, where they could safely—at least on the surface—be ignored by the ruling whites (however poor, however "foreign" those whites might be), and who, when Alex and I were children, were profoundly mysterious presences. Besides dressing differently and behaving differently, often they spoke little or no English. Our parents couldn't tell us their history; for the most part, our parents had no idea what it was, or maybe they didn't talk about the "Indians" out of some buried and unmentionable shame. So we children didn't understand who they were; we did not know what they did, or why they were there, or what we should think about them. We knew only the implicit judgement surrounding us that they were inferior.

Children such as Alex and I lived in mystery; it was all around us. What were the northern lights, those eerie lights in the twilight or night sky? And we were born into a resonant but frightening world of sound: the mournful cry of loons, the soul-shivering wail of the timber wolves, the babbling of the great flocks of geese going north or south depending on the season and filling the sky with their noise, the scream and battering of the snow-laden wind during winter storms, the trickling of water, or its splash and roar in the spring as streams swelled and became impassable. And for me, the fierce and terrifying whine of the bull saw at the sawmill my father ran, and for Alex, the more reassuring roaring *clank* of the old mechanical farm machinery, and the steady loud *chug* of the donkey engine that gave electricity to those of us who had one, but that, because they burned fuel and fuel was expensive, we ran for only a few hours each day.

That same wild and threatening forest, though, was full of interesting plants, from wild hazelnuts to berries of many different kinds, and we children knew these plants from forays with our mothers to pick them—saskatoons, chokecherries, blueberries—and sometimes wildflowers to brighten our log or frame shacks. The pastures and the ditches beside the makeshift roads were rife, in spring, summer, and fall, with many-coloured wildflowers: the red-coral of Indian paintbrush, the delicate mauve-tinged blue of bluebells and flaxflowers; in late summer and fall the glow of goldenrod, the brilliant black-dashed scarlet prairie lily—whole astonishing, enchanting fields of them in those days; in spring the purple of crocuses, not to mention the dandelion that showed its yellow face everywhere in the grass. And there were pussy willows and cattails and rushes and sedges growing in the bogs and swamps, and wild, deep-pink roses blooming profusely everywhere and scenting the already scented air.

We smelled the north; we breathed wildness in with every breath, and did not know that was what we were breathing; the brilliant, clear air of the north carried down to us through the arctic snows and ice, across the tundra, and the miles and miles of pine and spruce forest farther north of us. We could smell water—in those days, in those places, water was everywhere: in spring, small streams became rushing rivers, bogs and swamps grew wider and deeper, roads were destroyed, people were stranded by the water. Our fathers and brothers would fell more trees, slice them lengthwise (or not bother) and cover the offending mud-and-water-filled holes with logs neatly arranged perpendicular to the direction of the road—called corduroy roads—over which our horse-drawn wagons or our Ford Model T's could navigate without getting stuck.

But in autumn the forbidding, dark forest would transform to glowing gold, orange, yellow, and red that whispered and rustled and tapped softly to us. We lived in a world of light until the leaves fell, stripping the trees to their skeletons, covering the ground underfoot with a crackling carpet. Then the snow began to descend, the wind to howl around us, and winter arrived. The snow, mountains of it, never ceasing, never subject to the snow-eater wind, Chinook, but piling up and piling up all winter long until it seemed that we would all be buried alive under its ceaseless fall.

Yet winter had its own great beauty, with the sun or the moon shining on snow, causing it to glitter like fields of jewels, or change from white so bright you couldn't look at it to deep blue and purple, despite the danger of frostbite and worse, of freezing to death, of disappearing in a blizzard and not being found until spring. In those days, in that place, we had cold of such intensity and ferocity that those of us who lived through it—people like Alex and me—can't think of it except in mythical terms. Nobody raised up there in the days before reliable vehicles and down-filled parkas could ever forget what it feels like to be cold, dangerously cold, of freezing cheeks and noses and fingertips and toes, and the hurt of the thawing. Or memories of our fathers and brothers sitting on bare wooden kitchen chairs or pine benches, pant legs rolled up to their knees, their rarely seen and both comforting and startlingly large white feet resting in tin tubs of snow melted and warmed to tepidness and set on the bare plank floor, and in which their frozen toes were being slowly, painfully, brought back to life.

Work went on in winter too, though, including the chore of keeping the woodpile replenished with chopped lengths of trees to burn in the cookstove and the heaters to keep the house warm. I can still feel the weight of the loads too heavy for me to be carrying, so that after I had rolled them into the woodbox beside the stove, I had difficulty straightening my arms. If, after I'd taken off my parka, I bothered to push up my sleeve, my skin would be indented and pockmarked with red where the knots had been and the places where rough edges and bark had pinched my flesh. But through most of my childhood, wood had to be brought in and unlike Alex, who had six brothers, I had none; often my sisters and I were the wood-carriers.

This morning I sprinkled a handful of blueberries, bought at the store in town, onto my bowl of oatmeal. When I crushed the first one onto the roof of my mouth I remembered kneeling in sand somewhere in the north—outside of Nipawin, Saskatchewan, I think—in my homemade bib overalls and white cotton blouse, clutching a cup in one hand as I picked small, intensely flavoured blueberries from their low bushes. Somehow, in my memory there is always a pallisade or a high, peeled-log gate just ahead of me—I am guessing an entrance to a provincial park. It was—whatever the occasion—a happy time, it seems to me; no dark cloud hangs over that day. Of such were our northern childhoods made: berry-picking excursions, in good weather playing outside all day, listening (without realizing we were) to the birds and the animals, watching the ever-changing wild northern sky, using for toys sticks and branches and leaves and wildflowers and mud or clay and grass, and water, omnipresent and the most engrossing of all. I barely remember conventional toys; most of us had none, and didn't miss what we didn't even know about.

And the cooking! Our mothers and older sisters, our grandmothers and our aunts baked bread because there were no bakeries, they grew what vegetables they could and canned them, they picked berries and canned them, too, and they kept chickens and a milk cow and were expert in separating milk and making butter and cheese, and killing a chicken and preparing it for our supper. The huge amount of food the men consumed in those days, needing every calorie of it to offset the great number of calories they burned in their labours—labours which went on from before dawn until darkness fell and night lit its stars, and the northern lights—aurora borealis—began their pale pink, green, and white gossamer dance across the darkened, glowing sky.

All of this, Alex and I had in common as our first vision and knowledge of the world, and I cannot help but think that no matter what came after, where we went, the kind of education we were given, the future we imagined for ourselves had to have been deeply influenced by that very difficult, yet in some ways magnificent beginning—the beauty, the mystery, the intimate knowledge of the power of nature, breeding both a healthy respect bordering on terror, and an incurable awe. Whatever the specifics of our situation, Alex and I shared that northern pioneer beginning.

If anything contributed to the difficulty, beyond intractable nature itself, it had to have been our parents' belief in how the world should be, how it was in the places from which they had come. For my mother, a prosperous farm in southern Manitoba was paradise itself; for my father, it was an intimate connection with a settled and well-peopled French-speaking, Roman Catholic community. Alexandra's father had come as a boy from Ukraine with his own father, Stefan. His mother, Alex's grandmother, did not follow for some years, most likely until her husband had settled on some land and built, if not a full-blown house, at least a shelter that would withstand the winter, and until he had begun tilling his land, growing a crop that he could sell in order to have an income, at least partly to pay his wife's passage. Alex's parents and seven of an eventual ten children were driven from their first home at Rhein, Saskatchewan, by a five-year grasshopper infestation, which is how they settled at Endeavour—their second try.

Alex's oldest sister, Marie, tells me that their grandparents and their father came in 1912 from Chernovtsi, or at least, she remembers that he often mentioned that name. I assume he meant he had not come from the city, but from the *Oblast*, or region. (There is, or was, a large immigration hall in the city of Chernovsti, in the province of Buchovina, and because many Saskatchewan Ukrainian people came from it, today it is a sister city to Saskatoon.) Alexandra's mother was born in Canada, although she spoke little English and her children, even after they'd become fluent in English and accustomed to using it every day, continued to speak Ukrainian to her. What might have been paradise to them, I can only guess, had to have been land of their own, and enough of it, in a Ukrainian community, preferably Ukrainian Orthodox as the Wiwcharuks were.

How the world should be was not how it was. We weren't born in Ukraine or Quebec or anywhere else but where we were. What was, to our parents, the unfortunate present, fit only to be altered and repaired but never quite measuring up to the past, was in fact our only reality. Or it would have been our only reality, if our parents hadn't kept suggesting that the real world was elsewhere (that mysterious place from which they had come), or was in the future. Maybe all parents do that to some extent to all children, but for the children of pioneers it was virtually guaranteed that they would be taught that things as they were weren't good enough, and that the true home was elsewhere. And for us, the worst of it was that our parents had chosen to go places where creating the world they wanted wasn't going to be possible. Farmers at heart, all of them, even my father, would find there were too many trees, too many huge balls of roots, too much brush to be cut, piled, and burnt, and after the trees and brush were gone, too many stones, too poor a soil, too harsh winters, and too many biting insects the rest of the year.

Our family would be gone in a few years, my father having failed in his sawmill operation; Alex's family would hang on until she was in nursing school before they sold the farm and retired to that acreage outside of Saskatoon. My family left broke; Alex's parents left never having achieved the prosperity pioneers dreamt of. My memories would be forever tinged by my parents' memories of their failure. Struggling between my mother's dreams of elsewhere—an elsewhere I had never seen—and her hatred of the only place I knew, and my own not-quite-settled feelings about my first home, I would never think of that place without an aching bewilderment.

Perhaps the same wasn't true of Alex. She was fifteen when she left that small home farm, voluntarily, to go to high school in the city. She was the youngest, the last child to leave, according to the sister next to her, Ann, the favourite, and her parents remained behind for another six or so years on their farm. It had to have been simply home to Alex, and if there were bad memories too, as there always are in families—and hers was large, ten children—they were subsumed by her intense love for her parents, and by a primal sense of that world containing in itself the possibility of paradise. If I grew up never sure where home was, Alex would have had no doubt. If I grew up with an ineradicable insecurity about who I was, Alex would have been secure in that knowledge, even if, one day, wanting to claim a more glamourous background, she might choose to deny it.

I can't help but think about what that beginning meant to me: it may have prepared me to be a constant questioner, or if not to actually ask the questions out loud, to gaze around me, in a kind of confused surprise, with awe always behind my perceptions. If my first view of the world was was filled with a sense of the perilousness of life, of insecurity, and of great mystery that existed just beyond the skirts of my mother's housedress, this feeling would not vanish, but instead would form the basis of how I viewed the cosmos.

Surely Alex also must have had some of that same sense of the underlying danger and mystery of life, and of its precariousness: the precariousness of our households, our farms, our places in the world. We all knew that where our next meal would be coming from depended on the continuing goodwill and good health of our moms and dads; it depended on the weather. In those days we stayed alive because we were determined to stay alive, and because we were willing to work as hard and as long as was necessary.

Being a girl was a big part of it. Girls were expected to work as much as men, but they knew that the important work was done by the men, the hardest work, and that without the men we could not survive. I had my father, a couple of uncles, and my grandfather in my life. Alex had her father and six brothers, although by the time she was fifteen and ready to leave for the city, there would have been only her father left at home. The odd thing was that coming from such a world you did not feel yourself to be capable of anything, but instead felt the necessity of having strong, god-like men in your life.

We would be torn, all our adult lives, between the need to claim Ukraine or Ireland or France as our true home, and the recognition that our entire lives had been made and lived in Canada on the Western prairie. We dreamed that when the time came and we had earned the money, we would go back to our roots. It would be our attempt to make some kind of order out of the chaos that is the past and, thus, to make some sense of the present.

Now, looking back, I think it a fine metaphor: the wilderness of forest, rock, and swampy land standing for the unremembered, untamed past, which nonetheless formed us, formed our souls, formed also our idea of *home*, yet all of this unrecognized and unacknowledged, and not to be reclaimed as part of our real lives until we were old. For Alex, who didn't live long enough, never.

I think about the governments that opened that difficult land for settlement and found ways to encourage the unwary, the hopelessly romantic, or the desperate, to take their families there to try to forge an existence out of such wilderness. I detect a sense of personal superiority in remembering those politicians and civil servants: *It's good enough for them*, they seemed to think. *I wouldn't dream of doing it myself, and anyway, I have no need to because I have made a better life for myself than those poor dolts will ever do.* It makes me furious to think of it; it makes me furious to think of our claim that Canada is a classless society.

I was born in what had been a Red Cross outpost hospital in the town of Nipawin, a good thirty miles from our home in the bush—a distance, in those days, given the often impassable roads and the poor-quality vehicles we had, that was near impossible. But despite the difficulty, all five of us were born in hospitals.

Alex, born April 20, 1939, was the only child of ten to be

born in a hospital, in nearby Canora because Endeavour didn't have a hospital. Her mother had had some difficulty with her second-last birth (Alex's sister Ann, five years older), and everybody agreed that a hospital delivery would be safer for both Alex's mother, Aneta—or Anna, as she was mostly called—and for the new baby. In fact, although the birth was normal, Anna had a vision in which she saw her new baby suspended above her and with wings, an infant angel. She thought, for a few terrible moments, that Alex had died.

The Wiwcharuk family was embedded in that community: Alex's father, Alexander, was a ratepayer and one of those who helped to organize the school district and to build the school that Alex would attend when she was ready. It was called Bear School (no question about why), and it was two miles from the Wiwcharuk farm, a long walk for a little girl. She would attend it until she was ready to start high school; in fact, it would be 1959, a year after she had finished high school, before the town of Endeavour acquired a school large enough for all the country children to be bussed to, another measure of the remoteness and perhaps even of the poverty of the community. If Alexander Wiwcharuk did the things responsible men do in a new community—serving on boards, making decisions about public buildings and services—Anna did what the women did: cooking for community events, making arrangements for the welfare of the children who would attend them, helping the priest with his duties and making sure the church and the halls were clean and well-appointed, and that the children learned the church rituals and their prayers. There were plenty of relatives nearby—

aunts and uncles and cousins—and all of them living the same hard, determined, pioneer life.

It was wartime, too, that Alex and I were born into; it was the background to our lives. The men listening solemnly to an armchair-size radio set in the parlour or the living room, the women knitting or making bandages to be shipped off to "the front." The ration books were guarded as fiercely as the Bible, voices became hushed when children entered the room. And the strange events: a young man in his heavy khaki-coloured wool uniform and puttees, invited to supper at our log house, who sat motionless, booted feet placed neatly together on the bare wooden floor, face pale and drawn, hands folded on his lap (a picture that to this day, over sixty years later, I have not forgotten), as my mother and aunt moved around the kitchen making the meal, and them saying afterwards, when he had gone, *The war ruined him*, and us wondering what that appalling remark meant: our mother bustling us home angrily in the darkness from the ball diamond where a fire sent flames high above the backstop from a burning effigy of Hitler. When we asked if it was a real man on fire, she had bitter words for the young men who had spoiled the day—although I have no memory of what the day was.

My family had one advantage over the Wiwcharuks: we were already Canadians, had been on my father's side since the seventeenth century, and on my mother's since the early nineteenth. War and political oppression were not things we knew much about, it was all so far in our families' pasts, while the Wiwcharuks would have had in their family background all

too much of both. If we children were very glad that this mysterious event called "the war" was somewhere far away from
us, the Wiwcharuks must have been immensely grateful that
they had escaped it—both the second war and the first one.

During the First World War, six thousand Ukrainians
in Canada were interned, and any of them who had been
naturalized Canadians fewer than fifteen years lost the right
to vote. Alex's father had arrived as a child in 1912 and so
would have fallen under this ruling. Nonetheless, there were
a lot of Ukrainian Canadians who did, and it is quite possible that members of Alex's family, or at least some of their
neighbours, did. This has to be a part of Ukrainian-Canadian
lore, its history in this country, but I suspect that it is not
the first thing Ukrainian children are taught in those classes
they are sent to, or used to be when I was young, every Saturday morning, where they learned, among other things, to
read and write Ukrainian. The elders of an oppressed group,
judging forgetting to be the best way, don't always want their
young to know about such past discrimination. Nor would
they want their Canadian-born children to know about the
suffering they and their ancestors had endured in Ukraine,
nor family stories of who betrayed whom, who was tortured
by whom, who was hanged, or murdered, or went over to the
other side, back in the old country.

By the time the Second World War began, and Alex was
born, only new immigrants from Eastern Europe were forced
to report once a week to the local post office so that the government could keep tabs on them. But that must still have

rankled in the Ukrainian community, and left a residue of determination that children born in Canada would prove the value of the Ukrainian community by joining the middle class, and becoming full-fledged Canadians.

I'm struck now by the way that old people talk about those days, telling you not about the hardship, but about how much fun they had—about the schoolhouse dances and parties, about coming home after midnight under the stars in the horse-drawn sleigh and falling asleep and the sleigh tipping and everybody falling out into the snow, about the picnics with the homemade ice cream, and the sack races and the fiddle music. As if that is all they can bear to remember. Although one very old lady, resting in a chaise longue in the nursing home, a brightly coloured crocheted afghan drawn up over her fragile body, murmured to me, "There were too many babies," daring to say it out loud at last.

That is what Alex and I came from: from wilderness, and from physical hardship. But we also came from a reverence for education, at least for girls, who wouldn't inherit land and who might not be lucky enough to marry it. Our mothers didn't want us to marry it. They knew all too well what marrying land, at least in those days and in that place, would mean for us: a life of hard work, without frills, or holidays, or even the slightest touch of glamour. They wanted better for us, and they knew we would have to get that "better" on our own, out of our sheer determination. So that much, Alex and I also had in common. The good life, for girls, would be had elsewhere, and we would have to get it ourselves.

Still, I had been convinced when I began my hesitant search to find out what had happened to Alex that we hadn't had much in common other than being in the same high school at the same time. But my curiosity had to have been growing: I'd gone so far as to make a date to meet the retired police officer, the one I'd been told was "obsessed" with Alex's case, and I felt that I'd better go to that meeting equipped with more knowledge about who Alex was and what our connection may have been. That was why I visited our old high school, the Saskatoon Technical Collegiate Institute—now the board of education's offices, the school having been defunct since the seventies—to try to track down some yearbooks from 1954 to 1958, my own having long since disappeared.

I was lucky to find a room devoted to Tech memorabilia, and a cardboard box full of our old yearbooks. The woman who took me in left me alone with the box, and I searched through it for the books covering the years we were students there, while black-and-white photos of all our old "Senior Pins" and "Senior Rings" gazed down at me. (These were the student body presidents, one male, one female each year, whose symbol of office had been either a pin or a ring.) I recognized most of them, remembered something about them even if they hadn't been friends of mine. It was an odd sensation, sitting and flipping through those books while those young men and women hung, frozen in our mutual teenage past, all around me.

There she was—Alex—a teenager, staring solemnly out at the camera in most of the shots, black-haired, round-faced, with a pretty, well-shaped mouth as her distinguishing feature, and nearly black eyes. I found myself, too, and if I thought Alex was an amorphous-looking person, neither adult nor child, caught between two life stages, I thought this was even more true of me. That timid mouth, those dark eyes that seemed to see the world without certainty or love. I confirmed that Alex was the girl I remembered, that we had been in choir and drama club at the same time. Alex didn't seem to have done much in the way of extracurricular activities and I couldn't find any indication of her being a serious scholar or an athlete or anything beyond her drama club membership to distinguish her. Maybe I couldn't remember much because there wasn't much in the way of high school social life to remember. I could never say that I had had a successful time in high school, although I did have lots of good memories.

Bemused, satisfied to be a grown-up, I put the yearbooks back in the box and walked out of the building, not knowing it would be my next to last time in it. Back in my car, I did a quick review of my notes on the facts of her murder as reported in the newspaper. Although I was glad to be about to speak with somebody who'd been in a position to know a lot more about the murder and its investigation than a reporter would know, there is no denying that I was intimidated, and I already had a sense that I would be expected to be shrewd and capable. Feeling anything but, I was gearing myself up to give that impression.

I still have the notes I reviewed that warm afternoon sitting in my car: I see I'd also attempted to come up with some questions to ask, but really, I knew so little that my questions even then seemed silly and ineffectual. I see with some amusement that I hadn't even started a new notebook, as I always do when I start a new book, that the reverse side of the page on which I'd made my notes is covered with scribblings from a lecture I'd attended about the bedrock geology of Saskatchewan. Beneath my quick review of my notes was that abyss of my uncertainty. Why was I doing this? Strangely, I see now, there was a measure of childish glee at being taken so seriously. As if I had at last been accepted into the ranks of the adults. That was my mood when I took my first hesitant step toward discovering Alex's story.

# Chapter Three
## Being Ukrainian

Alex and I were raised in rural Saskatchewan during wartime and at the tail end of the pioneering period which so defined and shaped all of us, and the generation or two before us, in Western Canada. I thought of the things we would both have known when we first arrived in Saskatoon, the big city, the exciting place where our lives would finally begin. A pair of simple country girls—children, really—unacquainted with a need to be careful of or afraid of anything much but wild animals, with nature as enemy: the ice and snow of winter, swollen, wild streams, bogs and swamps. Country life had, has always had, a kind of transparency to it. We knew nothing of the way that cities, even small ones in the middle of nowhere, pull apart family life, sending each family member off in a different direction each day, each in some way and without meaning to, leading a secret life. I was thinking of how Alex and I grew up in this city, each in our separate ways.

Alex was wholly a Ukrainian girl, which is not to say that she hadn't been born in Canada, or had somehow escaped all

the influences of the English-speaking, Anglo–Saxon world
in which she was raised—in which we were *all* raised, even
half-French Canadian me. But, when we were growing up in
Saskatchewan, it was a much better plan to have an Anglo last
name such as Smith or Mc-something-or-other, instead of Le
Blanc—my own surname—or worse, the unpronounceable
Wiwcharuk, which was Alex's. Some Slavs bowed to the pressure and Anglicized their last names, including one of the men
initially suspected, but innocent, of Alex's murder and whose
Anglicized last name would cause endless trouble for him, link-
ing him, as it appeared to do, with a prominent Anglo family, and further confusing an already confusing investigation. I
notice in the Saskatoon phone book that some Wiwcharuks,
in an attempt to simplify the name, have dropped the second *w*,
which was the letter that tended to confound non-Slavs. And
after as much as one hundred years in Canada, why not such a
minimal concession?

But Alex had come from the Yorkton–Canora area, which
was one of the many areas where Ukrainians had settled in large
numbers around the turn of the century and where it was possible
to grow up speaking fluent Ukrainian, as she did, to be a devout
Ukrainian Catholic or Ukrainian Orthodox churchgoer, as Alex
was, and to be perfectly versed in Ukrainian culture, or at least that
which could be transported from Ukraine and maintained in the
face of some hostility and unspoken prejudice. Ukrainians in Saskatchewan take a tremendous pride in their Ukrainian heritage,
and over the years in Canada, they maintained it as they slowly
made their way from a position somewhere near the bottom of

the social ladder to one where they are able to boast a governor general (Ramon Hnatyshyn), two provincial lieutenant governors (Stephen Worobetz and Sylvia Fedoruk in Saskatchewan), and a provincial premier (Roy Romanow, 1991-2001), among their ranks of well-educated, middle-class professional people. Alex was of the generation that still suffered from prejudice, although it was lessening because most of her generation could speak unaccented English. But even someone as gifted as Roy Romanow, in high school in Saskatoon when we were, spent hours with a tape recorder when he was an adolescent working to rid himself of his Ukrainian accent, which he did so well that while still a teenager he was able to be a broadcaster at a Saskatoon radio station.

A Ukrainian woman also raised in Endeavour, but slightly younger than Alex, told me that in her hometown, "You always knew who counted and who didn't, and that the English (the Anglos) mattered and we didn't." We were drinking coffee in the kitchen of her big, bright, modern house, the kind of house our mothers would barely have been able to dream of, living as they did most of their lives in log houses and settlers' shacks, or the small houses I've described on the west side of Saskatoon, and then winding up in a single room in a nursing home with one red geranium or a flourishing African violet on the windowsill. She laughed wryly, adding, "Even though there were more of us than them." That she had married a relative of mine on my mother's side, perfectly British Isles in background, amused us both.

My half-French background didn't cause me any trouble that I can remember because we didn't speak French at home, and so I grew up without an accent, and because we hadn't a French mother, there seemed not to be anything identifiably French about us beyond our French surname. (And I was called Sharon, not Yvette or Germaine.) It was more of a problem to be a Roman Catholic, and my memories of discrimination were not the result of the French background—this wasn't true of my father, though, whose accent, which he never lost, gave him away—but of being poor and, especially, of being Roman Catholic. But, of course, to be a Slav was to be lower on the pecking order than to be half-French, and how could having a fixed place near the bottom of the social ladder not affect you for the rest of your life?

The thing about being Ukrainian or half-French or Chinese or whatever was that wherever you went, except when you were at home with your family, or gathered with other Ukrainians or Chinese at your church or at a cultural event, you were always Other, you were never quite the real thing, and you knew it. And no matter how much it chafed, there was also always a part of you that accepted that designation, and that yearned to be whole and real.

If I often felt it, despite my mother being the real thing—Irish on her father's side and Scottish on her mother's—how very much more Alex must have, as a child, how much she would have been forced back, again and again, for validation, into her own Ukrainian community. Even today, Roy Romanow tells of Anglo neighbours the Romanows had for many years who, despite being polite, even friendly, never—in all the years the two families lived next door to each other—

invited the Romanows into their home for lunch or dinner or even a cup of coffee. He told me this without rancour, but as an illustration of how it was to be a Slav in the Saskatchewan in which we all grew up.

Ukrainians settled the Yorkton area as early as 1897, but as the province's population began to urbanize—this trend, which goes on today, began even before the Depression of the thirties—Saskatoon also became a centre of Ukrainian culture and life. At its peak, its Ukrainian population was at something like twelve percent, and it stayed at about this level into the early fifties. This was out of a population of 53,000; but by 1956, only three years later, it was 73,000, a thirty-four percent jump. The bulk of the Ukrainian population lived on the west side, where I lived when we first came to the city, and where housing was cheap but decent. Most of the immigrants to the city, Ukrainians included, were working class people, and with their farms gone or abandoned, and without university degrees or the kind of training that city people tend to have available to them, the men supported their families by working for the railroads, or for the city or municipality as labourers, or in any number of other manual jobs a new city needed men to do. My own father was a mechanic in a series of garages. This hard work was to be the foundation on which all those country people would learn to live in the city, to take advantage of its schools and hospitals, its cultured and learned people who understood music and world literature and everything there was to know about science, and who would teach their children to be doctors, lawyers, artists, architects, and teachers.

But Alex's father had managed to hang onto the family farm, and so when Alex came to the city it was not with her mom and dad and siblings, but to live with her oldest sister, Marie, who had married a non-Ukrainian, a tall, handsome man with an Anglo surname, who ran a successful plumbing and refrigeration business. They lived in the Exhibition District, another of the areas where housing was relatively cheap and the lots small, and where families trying to establish themselves would often begin. Still, Alex and her sister's family had to go over to the west side to attend church. They were Ukrainian Orthodox, and the main church of the faith was the Holy Trinity Cathedral, which still sits, well kept-up and attractive and in full use, on 20th Street at Avenue J, another of those places I used to pass every day on my way to St. Mary's School. Alex's priest at the Holy Trinity Cathedral was Father Bodnarchuk.

The cathedral was (and remains) white stucco with one large green "onion" dome in the centre of the roof, and I found it less visually interesting than St. George's Ukrainian Catholic Cathedral on Avenue M between 21st and 22nd streets. That one has eight onion domes of different sizes and I remember many years later, when I taught at Princess Alex School, taking my grade eight art class to sketch the church. In fact, somewhere in the mountains of paper in my office there is a sketch book that includes my own unfinished attempt, from around 1970, to draw the cathedral.

The two Ukrainian cathedrals served two different religions, the Ukrainian Catholic and the Ukrainian Orthodox.

If I had tried to draw both cathedrals, I would have noticed at once that the Ukrainian Catholic church has straight-armed crosses on its domes, while the crosses of the other, the Ukrainian Orthodox church at Avenue J, have one arm set at an angle. One day I would visit Alex's grave, and there I would see the one slanted arm of the three on the cross that comprised her tombstone, proclaiming forever that here lay a Ukrainian Orthodox soul. (I'm told that the slanted arm is, among other things, a reference to St. Andrew, who was martyred on an X-shaped cross.) I knew when I saw that cross that I would have to make some, if only cursory, effort to understand her religion.

The truth is, I was always curious about Ukrainians and their religion and their customs. We all knew about Ukrainian Christmas—a lavish, twelve-course meatless meal beginning, famously, with cooked wheat soaked in honey, called *kytia*—and Ukrainian dancing was a marvel and delight, as were the colourful costumes, but I still felt there was some mystery about being Ukrainian, some magical depth to be plumbed. Now, I knew that to understand Alex I needed to know something about her culture. I was secretly glad to have an excuse to ask questions about the things I'd always wondered, but had never dared to ask.

Whenever I asked Ukrainian Orthodox church members about the two religions, they were adamant that they are different, that the Ukrainian Catholic is a branch of the Roman Catholic faith, and that the Orthodox religion is entirely separate from Catholicism, whether Ukrainian or

Roman. The differences are large: Orthodox priests are free to marry; the Orthodox use the Julian calendar and celebrate Christmas and Easter later in the year than Catholics do; the Orthodox do not accept the doctrine of the infallibility of the Pope as Catholics do; the two churches have two different hierarchies; and as well, they differ in traditional practices. (There are also more subtle theological differences, which I am too ill-equipped to go into.)

Of less significance to the Orthodox would be, for example, the dried palm branches, blessed by our priest, that my sisters and I would carry home from church on Palm Sunday, while Alex and her family would be carrying home pussy willows. The Orthodox faithful also hang icons in the home, often of the Virgin Mary, or of saints or other important scenes in the Orthodox story, and they keep a jar of holy water that has been blessed at the Feast of Jordan/Epiphany. We Roman Catholics had crosses on the wall, and maybe a religious picture or two, but icons would be as rare in our houses as they would be commonplace in Orthodox homes.

On April 30, 2004, a Saturday, I called to speak with Alex's eldest sister, Marie, about some of the dates in the family history. I asked her if I had called at a good moment, and she explained that it was, in fact, on the Julian calendar, the day between Good Friday and Easter Sunday and that she was very busy kneading her Easter bread, but that her husband would take over the task while she talked to me. We spoke for twenty minutes or so, having met some months earlier when she had gone to the trouble of coming to one of my readings and searching me out to speak to me. I asked her about the Easter-basket custom. She told me that she and her husband would fill four Easter baskets, one for each of their children, all grown now and with their own families living not too far from where she and her husband had retired.

First, she explained, the basket is lined with an embroidered cloth, perhaps made of linen, and hand-embroidered in colourful traditional Ukrainian designs. Next, the basket is filled with items such as home-baked Easter bread, usually of two varieties, sweet and plain, ham or sausages along with horseradish to be eaten with the meat, home-grown green onions, cheese (traditionally home-made cottage cheese), butter, hard-boiled eggs, cake or cookies baked using the dairy products which are not eaten during Lent, as well as candles to light during the blessing. Then the basket is decorated with Easter eggs, or *pysanka*, a traditional craft requiring great delicacy and skill (and one of the things my Ukrainian school friends—the girls—might have been learning when they went off to Ukrainian classes on Saturday mornings. I didn't know it until recently, but the designs are traditional too, and they each carry meaning). The finished baskets are then taken to church to be blessed as part of the Easter Sunday service.

It is at Easter also that when the carrier of the basket knocks on the door of a recipient and by way of greeting says to the occupant of the home, "Christ has risen," the occupant solemnly replies, "Indeed, He has risen." (In fact, this greeting is standard among the Orthodox during the Easter period. I first heard it from my husband's Slovak father.) After church the basket is taken to a family gathering, where the contents are shared as part of the celebration of the most significant event of the church year—as it is in the Roman or Ukrainian Catholic church.

But Alex and I had in common something more important, in church terms, than either of us would have realized: that was the veneration of Mary. The year I began grade eight at St. Mary's School on Avenue O, on Pleasant Hill, was a Marian Year. That is, a year singled out by the church fathers as one in which special reverence and honours were to be paid to Jesus' mother, the Virgin Mary. (Its purpose was also to celebrate the centenary of the papal definition of the doctrine of the Assumption—that at her death, Mary ascended, body and soul, to heaven.) She was everywhere, it seems to me now, her hands clasped, her head tilted downwards, her expression sad and gentle, her robes a beautiful blue. She was slender, beautiful, and distant, and although she was a virgin—in fact, according to Augustine, "a virgin ever virgin"—and that was important, I did not know what a virgin was. Nor was I at all sure what the prostitutes I saw every day on my way to school down 20th Street actually did, besides getting drunk, fighting, and hanging around with men. I did know that to be a prostitute was something dreadfully wrong, and to be a virgin—whatever that was—was the best thing of all to be. I knew, of course, that both of these had to do with men, even if I did not know precisely what.

During that year, 1954, there was constant talk of the importance of Mary and the place she should occupy in our spiritual lives, but mostly about her inseparability from God because she was Jesus' mother. We were not interested in theology, but the veneration of Mary was important to us, even if we did not fully understand the message. What it said was that women had value. Or, at least, sinless, pure women did.

If Mary was presented as a role model for us, I don't think any of us saw a way in which we might be like her, other than if we had a vocation to be a nun. Most adolescent girls in the fifties from average Canadian homes did not know how babies were conceived, or anything about contraception, and we didn't dare ask. And we were told that Mary did not suffer from original sin. This was the doctrine of the Immaculate Conception, an ancient belief but one not proclaimed officially until 1954, the year we began high school. As an adult, I took the doctrine of the Immaculate Conception to mean that Jesus had been conceived without intercourse between Mary and Joseph. Of course, central to her role is the dogma that despite being a mother, she remained a virgin. No one ever explained that to us and I see now that that was because to explain it would involve explaining sex, something we shouldn't know anything about until we got married.

Living on the west side as I did, and having to walk all the way down the avenues to O to go to school, we saw a lot of life that our parents—benighted, not understanding the city—knew nothing about. As little girls we were sometimes accosted by the drunks—always white men—hanging around in front of the four hotels with beer parlours, and their laughing attempts to touch us as, already wary, we dodged them, weren't any different than the grabbing of the boys we knew at school. At least, I believe that was what I thought, for having no clear notion about sex, how could I know about rape? Or pedophilia? Or about any of the true evils that were going on around me all the time in the place where I lived, and of which I saw manifestations every day and which I understood only in some sub- or pre-conscious way?

And we saw prostitutes—always white women at that time—behaving in scary, inexplicable ways. Once, on a city bus in the evening, I was going to an event at St. Mary's Church Hall, down 20th Street, when at the corner where one of the beer parlour–hotels sat, the few of us on the bus heard the raucous voices of women coming closer from down a side street, their shouts, and the clatter of their high heels on pavement. Then out of the darkness came a woman, running as fast as she could in her high heels and too-tight skirt, and chasing her, gaining on her, at least three other women, all dressed as she was and with shoulder-length dyed and curled hair and red, red lips and fiercely made-up eyes. As the first woman reached the lights of 20th Street, the bus driver, idling there at the bus stop, opened his doors and she leaped on board, muttered something to him, and, looking at none of us as we sat staring at her, plunked herself down on one of the seats near the driver, her back to us. While this was happening the other women reached the bus, but the driver, keeping the doors tightly shut, began to pull away from the curb. They pounded on the door and on its sides and then we were gone, out in traffic. It was over, and the woman sitting ahead of us began to subside physically, her shoulders lowered, her black, stiffly curled long hair began to gleam less ferociously, and as the blocks passed, she slowly became ordinary.

It was terrible and fascinating. If the very next morning I would go to church with my family and sit for an hour facing that statue of the Virgin Mary and hear again about her goodness, which was tied up in some baffling way with her virginity, and yet events like that of the previous night went on all the time, what on earth were the other girls and I supposed to think? The best way around this confusion was to pay no attention to what the Church said—except on Sundays, or when there was a priest, nun, or particularly pious relative around. So that is pretty much what we did.

Alex had better fortunes, having come to live in a better neighbourhood and with her older sister and husband who watched her closely. After she came to the city to live she probably saw only a tiny bit of what I saw. So it is fair to say that she was most likely more naive than I was, that she was better protected and felt in a general way safer in the world. She may also have been much more knowledgeable (although secretly, privately) about sex, because she had spent her whole life on a farm and all the farm kids knew things we city kids knew nothing about. Some farm parents would keep their daughters in the house when animals were mating, but that is not always predictable, and bulls, for instance, were always escaping their fields or corrals and mating with cows. But it is one thing to see animals mating and quite another to be seeing, and not understanding, prostitutes in their brutal, nighttime world.

I suppose the more practical difference between Alex and me when we were adolescent girls would be the wholeness of her family's faith and their cultural rootedness. With my French father and my non-French mother, my father's absolute Catholicism and my mother's ambivalence toward it, which sometimes bordered on hate, I could boast no such completeness. If Alex found herself Other only when she was not with Ukrainians, if she was Other in terms of mainstream Canadian life by virtue of the power of British influence, I seemed to be Other most of the time: French when everybody else was English, English when everybody else was truly French. Where to turn for proof that one existed and was real? I would spend many years learning that I alone would have to, first, find and define my true self, and then use it for validation. But Alex would always know that the Ukrainian-Canadian world was wholly hers if she wanted it.

All of this would be background to the world in which Alex became a young woman, a rich, complicated, often tragic history beginning in Ukraine a thousand years earlier, baggage which young people want to shed but which, in later years—years Alex was not to have—they find the need to reclaim. Not just reclaim, but study, and try to make their own. One day, I would do this too, with my own history. But when I was young, I thought I could simply toss all that past aside and create myself as whoever I wanted to be. There is evidence Alex thought that too.

❋

I was heading out to see the retired police officer who was "obsessed" with Alex's unsolved murder. I was nervous, but my curiosity was greater than my nervousness. And I was not afraid, not then. Why should I be? I was hoping that during our interview I would begin to see what the story was, what the angle would be, so that I could start thinking about a book. It was that possibility that drove me, above all others.

He had brought his wife, and eventually a second retired officer joined us. We chatted informally; I summarized what I had found in the newspaper—this was to show them that I'd done my homework, that I wasn't a sensation-seeking idiot—and we talked a bit about whether Alex had known her killer or not. The two former police officers seemed to lean toward thinking she *had* known him—or perhaps that there was more than one killer—and I said that I thought so too, although my comment was based on nothing but a sudden intuition. I didn't even know then how much I didn't know.

Never having had anything to do with police work beyond being an occasional reader of Agatha Christie and eventually P.D. James and John Grisham, I had no idea how convoluted a murder investigation could be, no real idea about things such as the corruption in police forces or in government—financial corruption, yes—other than what the popular media might have to tell us. I was just glad to meet these two men, anxious to talk to them, eager to listen to what they had to say about Alex's murder. Which, in the end, was not much. But the effect on me was huge: the first man's genuine pain, his anguish over his force's failure to solve the case (at least, that was how I interpreted the undercurrent of emotion I felt coming from him) reminded me that police officers are, first of all, people, husbands and fathers and citizens; the second man's not-very-deeply-buried anger, that I, just another bloody journalist, was going to start mixing in where I had no business to be.

I asked some questions based on rumours I was beginning to hear from the few people I'd contacted before our meeting, people who were high school friends and who had also known Alex. Did I know that she was pregnant? Or that she had been promiscuous? But when I quoted these to my new acquaintances, they said that none of them were true. At one point, one of the men, staring into the distance with a pained look on his face, said "If this were a TV show, it would turn out to be a cop who killed her."

"Oh, no, a conspiracy of cops," I said, laughing, and he laughed too. (Later, I would think that no television show about the investigation of a murder would be complete, either, without the second man's hostility.) We talked a little more about who might have killed her, drank our coffee, promised to meet again, and I went away having made my decision to follow Alex's footsteps on that fateful evening. I had no idea why. It just seemed like a good thing to do. Maybe I was trying to respond to this troubling sense I had of not knowing her, not having a grasp on anything about her or about her death. I wanted to walk my way into the past. I had a peculiar feeling that is hard to express: it was of something dawning in me, something bright and clear, something huge. Was it the opening of life for me, at last? Of real life? I think now that it was. But I did not know how hard that opening would eventually be.

And so I went to pay my first visit to Alex's grave in Wood-lawn Cemetery. The cemetery was close to where she had died, although that didn't occur to me at the time. I stopped at the small office to ask for her location—such a huge cemetery, more than fifty-five thousand people buried in its ninety-four acres since its opening in 1906. I found her near the road, in an older part of the cemetery where the trees, elms mostly, are old and thick and tall, and cast a beautiful shade across the rows of stone markers, and the smooth, grass-covered graves. Her headstone, of thick white marble veined with grey, was in the form of a Ukrainian cross, with not one, but three horizontal bars, the lowest one angled. It was a small headstone, but a beautiful and feminine one, perfect for the girl I remembered her as being. And I thought with what love she must have been buried, to have had so perfect a stone chosen for her.

A small, oval-shaped glass embedded in it held a coloured portrait of her, the one taken when she graduated from nurs-ing school, where she is smiling over her shoulder, her nurse's cap with its single black band perched on the back of her head, and her nurse's navy wool cape open and resting on her shoulders, and holding a bouquet of roses. In those days, all graduate nurses received that huge bouquet of deep red roses. I imagined their scent wafting upward as she held still for the photographer. I imagined her happiness. Below the picture, her name was chiselled in English: *Alexandria Wiw-charuk, April 20, 1939*, and below that, *May 18, 1962*. Farther down her name was carved again, this time in Ukrainian, with most of the letters still recognizable, but a few that had become hard to decipher.

In a later interview, Roy Romanow pointed out to me that her name, Alexandra, in the Ukrainian-Cyrillic version which I had painstakingly, though awkwardly, copied into my notebook and shown him, was spelled differently than in the English version. I remember, also, being startled to find faded plastic flowers on her grave, as if I had expected that no one in the world but me remembered her. I assumed her family, about whom I then knew nothing, must have laid the flowers, but then, I wondered, dismissing it at once as a ridiculously romantic notion, whether perhaps her murderer had. (Later, it occurred to me to look in the phone book, where I found a number of people with her last name, some presumably her relatives.)

This was an old part of the cemetery, and all the graves had the same smooth covering of dark green, well-tended lawn. I felt little at her grave except a mild puzzlement that such a savage end could result in the same well cared-for grave as the ones around hers belonging to those who had died more mundanely of heart attacks, strokes, pneumonia, cancer, accidents, or even peacefully in their sleep. I lifted my head to watch the traffic droning rapidly down Warman Road beside the cemetery. Its presence seemed to say that dying, however you might do it, would never leak into the world beyond the grassy verge of the cemetery.

After that, my resolve firmed, I drove to the address where, when Alex vanished, she had been sharing a basement apartment with three other nurses. The small apartment block at the correct address looked too modern to me, and I concluded that the one she had lived in must have been torn down. When I realized this, I didn't bother to get out of my car, but drove on to the drugstore nearby. At that time, it had been called Mead's, and the newspaper reported that it had been her destination when she'd left her apartment in order to buy stamps and to mail two letters she'd been carrying. One of the people I'd phoned earlier had claimed to me that she'd been carrying a make-up kit (and how odd that was, if all you were going to do was sit on the riverbank and had to go to work right away, anyway), and someone else that her hair was in curlers. The truth was she carried two letters from home, possibly her wallet, and at Mead's Drugstore she stamped and mailed the letters, and after that, it is thought, she carried only her wallet.

The drugstore had been modernized and had new owners and, again, I didn't go in. Instead, I parked nearby, because I wanted to go to the site where her body had been found in its first shallow grave in the sand along the riverbank, beyond the weir and the CPR bridge, themselves only a mile and a half downstream from our old high school. I got out of my car and began to walk down the worn and cracked sidewalk, falling into a reverie. As I walked a feeling of such familiarity overcame me that it seemed, for one moment, as I gazed down at the cracks in the sidewalk and at the few straggling blades of grass growing in them, that somehow over the many years Saskatoon had been home to me, and during the more than thirty years I had lived elsewhere, I had become this sidewalk.

I might live elsewhere, I might grow old, the city itself might change and expand and in parts be unrecognizable to me, but this old, crumbling, comfortable part of the city was inseparably a part of me—there was no Saskatoon without me—we were each other. And I thought, *how could I ever want to return here when every step reminds me of my early life, of some part of my personal story, all the bad parts of it?*

I lifted my eyes then and saw ahead of me, growing on the riverbank a few yards downstream from the weir, a cluster of elms, willows, and maples. I hadn't brought the newspaper description of the grave's location with me, that is, of how many yards it had been from the intersection, and from the weir, and how close to the CPR bridge, but I crossed the street, heading for the bluff of trees. I did not want to enter them, but I did, and standing among them, so close to the water below, whether I'd found the site of her murder and grave or not, I felt a shiver of horror, the first I had experienced since the moment, many years earlier, when I had first read of her death. And yet, it felt unreal to me, more of the kind a horror movie might induce, and I wondered at my own insensitivity.

I climbed back to the road, still uncertain as to whether I'd been to the right place, and went back to my car, where I sat a while, collecting my thoughts. It was only then that I was jolted by the realization that I had done all of this on the eighteenth day of May 2001, that is, on the thirty-ninth anniversary of her death. It felt to me that she had spoken to me from her grave, and was telling me that she was counting on me, that her soul still craved satisfaction, that I could not stop worrying until the police named her murderer.

If he had been as young as fifteen in 1962—about as young as we can conceive of a murderer being, although of course there are child murderers—in 2001 he would have been only fifty-four years old. Or he might have been in his sixties. He could have been living an ordinary life. I might even have known him or had friends who would have known him.

I started my car again and began the long, five-hour drive home, my heart feeling too large for my chest. I was deeply touched at that revelation of place I had experienced, satisfied that I had accomplished so much, even following in Alex's footsteps on the evening of her death, and disturbed and uneasy at my belated recognition of Alex's murderer as a real human being—and one who was probably still alive.

I believed then that murder was always out of madness, no matter what the courts said, or what people believed. I couldn't conceive of murder done out of perfect sanity. Even now, all these years later, I find myself pondering whether there really is such a thing as a cold-blooded killer. Why couldn't a murderer or murderess kill in the sanest moment of his or her life? After all, we recognize meanness in a person—somebody who is mean enough, we say, to snatch candy from a baby, to take what he wants without concern for the person he robs; is it the same kind of person who tortures? And why couldn't that meanness apply also to murder? Isn't meanness just a continuum? When I met the two policemen, I hadn't yet given any serious thought to the mind of a murderer, beyond my unexamined notion that murder itself was madness. That murder was always evil I took as a given, but how madness and evil were related, or if they were, was a question I had always found easier not to think about.

The police officers had suggested I try talking to the Saskatoon Police Service, and that seemed like a reasonable idea to me. They thought reading the autopsy report would be a good starting point as well, and to do that, I'd need to ask the police, or else the coroner's office.

I thought that enough time had passed since Alex's death that the police might be willing to talk about the evidence they had gathered, something about their suspects at the time, and maybe about the way the trail of clues had gone dead on them. I thought that they might see my interest as an opportunity, a conduit, to try one more time to find Alex's killer through my reminding people about the murder, I thought that somebody's memory just might be jogged about some vital detail so far missed, or that maybe somebody knew something, had known something since 1962, and would feel guilty enough, as a result of whatever I decided to write, to at last tell the authorities— and that would lead to the killer's capture.

I thought, too, on that day that had turned out to be the thirty-ninth anniversary of her death, that a goodly part of the continuing memory of Alex and her unspeakable end came out of not knowing exactly what had happened to her, and imagining how bad it must have been.

I remember clearly my initial reaction to the news of the finding of her body. When I opened the newspaper, the story occupied a whole page, maybe more, and there were black-and-white photos, and a big headline, CORPSE FOUND IN SHALLOW GRAVE IDENTIFIED AS MISSING NURSE; and below that, CLOTHING WAS THAT WORN BY MISSING NURSE, ROOMMATES TELL CORONER'S JURY. One photo was of three men, one in uniform, the other two wearing overcoats and fedoras and identified as Sergeant Major Tom Hession, Detective Inspector Giles Lee, and Police Chief Jim Kettles. It seemed to be night, and they were standing at the edge of a copse of trees much taller than they were, and staring down into an area at the foot of the trees that is black in the photo.

The second picture was of Alex's mother and father, her father looking at a large, framed photo he holds, I assume of Alex, while Alex's mother, sitting beside him, had closed her eyes. Both of them were solemn, her father revealing maybe a touch of anger in the set of his strong jaw, and her mother seeming, if anything, to be praying—praying perhaps for this moment to end. Her body seemed relaxed, as if she had always known it would come to this. Her hands were in her lap, her right hand seemingly picking at her left, which was lifted so that the palm half-faced the camera. Her hands seemed large, and strong. The last photo was of Alex as she smiled, over her shoulder at the camera, wearing her nurse's uniform and cap. This may have been the one that thirty-nine years later I would see sealed in full colour on her white marble headstone.

I stared at the photos in disbelief and amazement; I may

have read a few words, rapidly skimming the headline. I lifted my head and said to my husband (we would have been married less than a year then of the fourteen it would be before our divorce), my voice not much louder than a whisper: *"I knew her; I knew her."* I remember that I let go of the newspaper, and it slid off my lap onto the floor. It was not that I disbelieved the newspaper report; it was only that I was having trouble absorbing it. Was this the same Alexandra Wiwcharuk I had known? I looked at the picture: Yes, it was the girl I had known, although now surprisingly pretty. I began, *"But how—"* before I gave up whatever I was trying to say. I suppose I meant, how could she get killed? Not specifically, was it by a gun or a knife, but *How could such a thing happen? How could it happen to a girl just like me, to someone I knew? How could it happen here, in Saskatoon? Now?*

And that was about it. I read the report carefully, and I probably read it one more time after that just to make sure I wasn't dreaming. Then I put the paper away and headed out to do whatever it was I did in those days—I probably went to my summer job. I have some vague memory of that same night driving to the site, for whatever reason people do things like that—for the thrill of it, to try to make real what had happened, to be able to say that one had been there—but when we reached the end of 33rd Street and saw the several hundred people standing on the riverbank or parked in their cars staring out to where Alex had been killed, we grew embarrassed, faintly ashamed, and instead of stopping, drove on by. I think I phoned at least one and maybe two of the girls with whom we'd attended high school, but although one of them knew Alex had gone on to nursing school, neither of them knew any more than I did about her or her murder.

I remember debating about whether I should go to her funeral or not. I had been taught that you don't go to funerals of people you don't know well; that is in bad taste; worse, it is a violation of a family's privacy. (Little did I know that one day I would live in a rural community where everybody went routinely to everybody's funeral; it was expected, as well as a social occasion.) Also, I had a job which I needed badly—I'd decided to go back to university that fall for my fifth year and my husband would be returning too—and I didn't dare risk losing it by asking for time off to attend a funeral for someone who was not an immediate family member. So I didn't go, and I don't remember ever regretting that I didn't go.

Now, looking back after all these years, I can only wonder at the mildness of my reaction, or non-reaction, to the news of such a shocking death of someone so young, someone I had known. I think now that it was the same reaction as that of others: I was just so stunned by this unprecedented event—and I do mean unprecedented—that I couldn't get a mental grip on it. I think that I was waiting, everybody was waiting, for the police to make the expected announcement: that they had caught her killer, that this was his name, this was why he had killed her, and exactly how, and that he would spend the rest of his life in prison. We were all waiting to hear that news, and expecting that when we did, we would be all right. We would gradually forget about it. But that news didn't come when it was expected, and it didn't come, and as I write this nearly forty-five years later, it still has not come.

But I think now that there was more to my lack of reaction, or to my stunned incomprehension, than I understood. Surely I was as frightened as were all the women who, forty years later, when I began asking questions, told me about their fears, about how they wouldn't go out unless there was a group of them, how they would call young men they didn't even know who lived in the apartment below them, or next door, to be their escorts if they had to run short errands in the same neighbourhood, how they padlocked their doors, or pushed furniture up against them, slept with butcher knives under their pillows or next to their beds, or couldn't sleep at night at all, and so on.

Some people, of course, felt differently. When, in 2005, I called Bill Davenport, who attended high school with Alex and me—his picture had been one of those hanging on the wall in the room full of Tech memorabilia—and who has lived in Saskatoon most of his life, he told me the story of how he had been playing bridge in the campus student union building with some friends on the day the news was released that Alex's body had been found. One of the men, who didn't know her, had not heard of her until the moment he heard of her murder, remarked casually that Alex had to have been promiscuous, wild, and that—the implication was clear—she could only expect what had happened to her, that in a sense, she had had it coming.

But the one woman playing cards with them, who also did

not know Alex, flared up in anger. "What right have you to say such a thing about a girl who has been raped, battered, and murdered? How do you know that? You don't know it; you don't know her. She isn't guilty of anything. She was *murdered*."

By this time it was early in 1962, and what was unusual about this exchange was not that the male student had dismissed Alex's death by blaming it on her but that the woman student had immediately defended her, hadn't let the man get away with his blithely scurrilous assumption about a woman he had never so much as met. In the fifties, we might have disagreed with him, but I doubt we would have challenged him—not about a woman we didn't even know. Maybe, in our innocence, we would even have drawn the same conclusion, thinking, if you obeyed all the rules, did what you were told, were very careful, nothing like that would ever happen to you.

Bill told them that he had known her, had attended the same high school for four years.

"What was she like?" they asked.

"She was quiet," Bill said, in his calm, low-key way. "She was a nice girl. Attractive. Anything but promiscuous—at least, not in high school." He couldn't believe that she had changed that much in a few short years; he didn't believe that she had had anything but a terrible misfortune.

As if simple fear resulting from what had happened weren't enough, there were pranksters out there, or maybe sadists, doing their best to frighten the already frightened. A girl who'd been in my class at St. Mary's in 1953-54 and whose picture I still have of the two of us and a third girl standing on

20th Street, wearing our Girl Guide uniforms and smiling and squinting into the sun, told me via another one of our gang of girls that in May 1962 she had been working at an office in Saskatoon. "We didn't have a switchboard in those days. And some guy with a creepy voice phoned and said that I'd better be quiet or I might get it next, or something like that." She wasn't the only one to receive such a phone call, which added to the general level of fear among the city's young women. In contrast, I remember feeling that it all had nothing to do with me, that it had happened in some other universe, that it was an event so out of line with normal existence that it was a fluke. That there was nothing to be afraid of.

I wasn't yet twenty-two, nobody I loved had died, I hadn't experienced any real catastrophes. My heart was unscarred. I didn't even think that I should shed a tear for propriety's sake. I thought, instead, fiercely, that to do so would be hypocritical. I had already developed the thick wall between the real world, the world of the heart, and the world of the mind, a capacity that universities teach the young. Or at least, which they taught them then. I had, as it is said, a lot to learn.

The existence of serial killers hadn't yet become a part of the lore of what it is to be a North American. We had little idea of somebody routinely hanging out in shopping malls looking for prey, or following a lone woman in a car to her destination, or waiting in bars until another victim came along. If we thought, in our sudden paranoia, that if Alex's killer killed once he might kill again, we thought so more as a result of watching movies and reading murder mysteries than any sense of there being men who enjoy killing again and again and again until finally they are caught. If we were afraid, it was not out of a strong sense of the evil of which humans are capable, demonstrated throughout history; it was more an atavistic fear, the fear that even modern women seem to have of the physical power of men.

The suggestion from the two retired police officers that the police would be willing to talk to me about Alex's murder came as no surprise to me; without thinking about it for a moment, I simply assumed they would. I took it for granted that the police were as upset as the public over the failure of their predecessors (who were all retired or dead) to catch her killer, and just as sure that once they saw that my interest was altruistic, that within limits (such as never naming a suspect or giving me whatever details crime novels say the police withhold in order to identify the killer), they would be willing to talk to me about their investigation. I was pretty naive the day I made my first phone call to the police service. Actually, I made several calls, and the officer in question always returned my call, but in each case would tell me nothing that wasn't already in the public arena. Talking to the officers seemed, to me, to be utterly futile. By the time the then new police chief, Russell Sabo, phoned one Sunday afternoon with the name of yet another officer I should call, I didn't bother. But there was still the coroner's report which might be had through the coroner's office, or so I thought, and there was

the board of police commissioners and—why not?—the Freedom of Information Act to apply to.

Besides this, I had been told by a former investigative
reporter that he'd been told by the former police chief, Dave
Scott, around 1995, that the police service had had a suspect all
these years, and that with the new DNA technology, they had
hopes of identifying Alex's killer fairly soon. But this was now
2001, and no such person had been caught. During this period
beginning in 2001 and through most of 2002, I was phoning,
writing letters, and applying to the freedom of information
commissioner, all more or less at the same time.

There were two more men still alive, former police officers, I was told, who had also had something to do with the
investigation of Alex's murder at the time it happened, and
so I called each of them. Their responses, in one case after
a couple of friendly phone conversations, and in the other,
immediately, in response to my asking for an interview, were
so deliberately rude, so abrupt, and so similar—*Not interested!
No! I won't be here!*—that I was stunned. Not even a polite
explanation about why they didn't want to talk to me? And
why, after friendly, even excited conversations earlier with one
of them, was I suddenly apparently afflicted with the plague?
*"Do you think somebody got to them?"* an acquaintance asked,
when I told about this baffling development more than forty
years after the murder.

I began to think that if no one who knew facts would talk
to me, it just might be because he had something to hide. But
I was coming to know that nobody official would give me

information because I was seen as a journalist, not as a citizen, or a friend of the murdered—as somebody who had no inherent right to information.

Knowing nothing about police procedures (except what I had seen on television and in movies or read in murder mysteries), or about the brotherhood of police officers, or about what I would begin to see as their arrogance, which smacked of a hard anger at the people they were hired to protect, not only at the criminals, I had never expected such absolute refusal. I hadn't for a second believed that there would be anything for them to hide. I had entered the world of question-asking in complete innocence. It didn't matter, in the end, if they returned my calls and treated me with cheery condescension, if they told me nothing that wasn't already in the realm of public knowledge. It didn't matter how charming they were, or how businesslike, if their main purpose was to make sure not one bit of information not already on the public record came to me.

When my application to see certain documents under the Freedom of Information Act came back refused, having already fully expected that, I barely read the formal justification, but the commissioner went to some lengths to try to help me, making it clear to the police that one of them had to talk to me. I didn't bother to apply to the court to have the ruling rescinded, because I was sure I wouldn't have a hope. My attempt to get hold of a copy of the autopsy report, via the office of the chief coroner, was equally futile. I was told, eventually, by a clerk, that all documents before 1970 had been destroyed in either a flood or a fire, I've forgotten which. (A few years later I would be given a copy and told it had come via the office of the chief coroner, that the chief coroner had decided to release it.)

But then I'd remind myself of something that in my frustration and anger I would keep forgetting: that it was never my intention to try to solve that forty-odd-year-old mystery. It was my intention only to write the definitive book about what had happened to Alex. When I was refused information, after I had shrugged off the humiliation, I just tried hard to think of another place where information might be found.

I also wrote a letter to the mayor at the time, who was Saskatoon's former police chief and chair of the board of police commissioners, which I copied to the then provincial justice minister, asking not for information about the murder, but that the investigation be "reignited and vigorously pursued," and telling them that I was most distressed about the failure to achieve justice for Alex. The murder and investigation was now either a "case," or a "file." Not the story of the horrifying act of violence that had killed a beautiful young woman just as her life was blossoming. Not the story of justice failed, justice not done. I kept thinking that it was only because all the people of whom I was asking questions were men that they could talk in that infuriating way about Alex's death. But then I caught myself calling it a "case," too.

I received a prompt reply saying my letter was being forwarded to the current chief of police, and only a week or so later, a letter came dated September 7, 2001, from a superintendent of police, saying, "This homicide is still open and active . . ," and, "I assure you that homicide files remain open until they are successfully concluded." I look back now and see that I hadn't asked for information. What I had really wanted, I remember, was for the board of police commissioners to have a letter in hand with regard to the murder and investigation, which would then make it possible for board members to request to see the file, something I'd been told that they could not do otherwise. This would then take it out of the tight fists of the police. I have no idea whether the board ever saw my letter, although it was addressed to them as well as to the chair.

It had been nearly thirty years since I'd last lived in Saskatoon by the time I was butting my head against all those stone walls. The Saskatoon Alex and I had lived in had been a very different place. Not just smaller, but, in my mind, run then by a handful of men, real personalities: Tommy Lennon, the "singing fire chief," James Kettles, the police chief, Sid Buckwold, the mayor and one of the smoothest and most charming men the city (at the very least) has ever seen. Tommy Lennon and Jim Kettles both had reputations as drinkers, and both had *opinions*, which they didn't hesitate to voice at any opportunity. Jim Kettles gave public radio addresses at Christmas, just like the Queen, and in them he tended to thunder out all the ways in which the citizens of the city failed to meet his expectations. He held views no public figure could get away with voicing today.

They ran a city that was growing so fast it must have been hard to keep tabs on everything that was going on. Between

1950 and into the eighties the city grew by about 20,000 people every five years. When Alex and I started high school it had a population of around 50,000 and when we finished, it was 56,000. By 1961, when I was still in university there, and Alex had returned to work at City Hospital, it had doubled in size to over 100,000, or a gain of more than 42,000 people. When we arrived in the city in the early fifties it didn't have a single shopping mall or a freeway. When we graduated in 1958 there had been no school killings—no Columbine, no *École Polytechnique*, no Dawson College—no mass murders other than the Holocaust, a full understanding of which we were still trying to absorb, and no serial killers we knew of beyond Jack the Ripper in late-nineteenth-century London, England. We still believed in a righteous war against evil killers such as Hitler, and unquestioningly in the heroism of our soldiers. There was no Vietnam, no Desert Storm, no Afghanistan, and no Iraq (never mind Chechnya, Rwanda, the killing fields of Cambodia). No *disappeared*. No terrorists, no World Trade Center. No soldiers murdering their prisoners or torturing them, especially not Canadian soldiers. The innocence of the average young Canadian—other than for the incomprehensible but terrifying atomic bomb and the truly incomprehensible hydrogen bomb, and the deliberate murder of six million Jews—was otherwise pretty much intact. Even corruption in governing bodies was considered to be unusual and very limited; corruption belonged to gangs, to the mafia, to the criminal element in general. Everybody else, we thought, could be relied upon to be honest.

But I remember an incident that happened around 1960. One night I was out with the man who would become, a year later, my first husband. Another couple was with us, when one of the men suggested that we should go for a drink to a boot- legger's establishment in downtown Saskatoon. It was nearing midnight on a beautifully warm and calm summer night. I remember that I was adamant that I would not go to such a place, that I would not go inside, that I wanted nothing to do with the idea. But we all got in the car and started driving across the city, and nobody backed me in my determination not to go, so that I gave up my objections, gritted my teeth, and nervously resigned myself.

When we got to the house in question—it was on 2nd or 3rd Avenue at the north end—we parked the car a half-block or so away. (I seem to remember that the man whose idea it was had been told not to park in front of the house itself so as not to attract attention.) A large, middle-aged woman sat on the front steps, smoking, in the soft darkness, and across the street a young constable walked with a measured gait toward the north, not looking across the street to where we approached the front steps. The woman said, "Shh. He's paid off, but if you make too much noise, he'll have to do something." By this time, steeped as I was in Hemingway, Faulkner, Nathaniel West, and dozens of other male American writers, I wasn't exactly surprised. Nor did I entirely believe her, being by that time well acquainted with the self-aggrandizing impulse. She told us to come in by the back door, and so around we went, climbed a few steps, and entered the brightly lit kitchen.

We were the only patrons there. It was a small house with a half-storey above us, and the two rooms I would see were almost bare of furniture, and if shabby, very clean. A young woman stood at the kitchen counter, and she turned and told us to go into the next room, the living room, where we sat on a couple of worn and lumpy sofas. One of the men told her what we would like to drink, paid for it, and then joined us. A moment later the woman came in carrying our drinks on a tray. I remember only that she was young, probably about my age, had long dark hair, was not especially pretty, but neither was she plain, but that she wore a sleeveless blouse and the shortest black shorts I'd ever seen, that her long, shapely legs were bare and she wore black high heels. Naive as I was, I knew I was in no position to make a judgement about how she was dressed, much as it shocked me. I remember watching her through the doorway as she went about getting our drinks, and that she was humming to herself, even doing a few dance steps, and I wondered what she was happy about, never thinking that this was a performance designed to attract customers, and not only to buy drinks from her.

Did someone tell me she wasn't really or only a waitress, but a prostitute? Or did I figure it out myself? What struck me most about her was that she was an attractive young woman, and why she would be a prostitute if she was attractive baffled me. One of the men said, surprised by my response, "If she weren't attractive, nobody would go with her." *What?* I must have thought. All the prostitutes I'd ever seen were on 20th Street, where long years of abuse, neglect, and alcohol had long since removed any traces of beauty, if there ever had been any. I'd equated ugly-and-worn-out with "prostitute," and it took me a long time to accept that pretty, shapely women might choose that life. I hadn't yet figured out, either, the world being what it is—what it *was* even then, although I had no idea of it—that many women who might have thought they chose to be prostitutes were in fact set up for it by the circumstances of their home lives, by the failure of institutions to protect children, by the downright evil of others.

Occasionally, also, I think of the gangly young policeman patrolling the sidewalk in the shadows across the street from us, and of the woman's claim that he had been "paid off." I wonder if it was true, and if so, was it strictly a deal between him and the woman, or did the corruption start higher up? And if it started higher up, then how wide was it? How far would the corruption extend in assisting criminal activities which tended, on the whole, to support men, and to disadvantage, to devastate women? I was realizing that the "amusing" events I knew about that had gone on in our city when I was young—the ones I'd seen myself, or the ones that "everybody" knew about—were not all that amusing and harmless after all, but were a part of what I was now beginning to think of as ordinary, everyday evil.

Before Christmas 2002, I had given up efforts on my own part to find out information about Alex's murder and the investigation and I had called the CBC investigative television program *the fifth estate*. To my surprise, one of the hosts, Linden McIntyre, returned my call and indicated interest in doing a program. Then, in January 2003, our phone rang around two in the morning, causing me to leap out of bed and groggily answer the first of several calls from someone I would come to know as a renegade. He was a retired police officer, one younger than I was, who had once been a homicide officer, and who called to give me some information or else to offer me advice on where to find more, or just to chat in a private way about what he knew about Alex's murder and its investigation. The upshot was that I heard things I would never, ever have heard otherwise. When I spoke on the phone to Linden McIntyre himself, as nearly as I can tell, it was those unsolicited and faintly sinister phone calls that persuaded *the fifth estate* to take on Alex's story.

In February, after having made arrangements to go to Calgary to spend two weeks studying French, my husband and I set out together, leaving our house locked and empty. He would drive me, stay a night or two, return home, and then come back to pick me up near the end of my course. As soon as he returned home, he called to let me know he had arrived, and that was when I began to realize that our phone had been tapped. It was just a clunky, obvious, voice-activated tap, otherwise I would never have known about it, but it was a tap nonetheless. Of that, I was sure.

At about the same time, just before Christmas 2002, an ex-convict (he said he had done fourteen of sixteen years in prison in maximum security jails, that is, fourteen years of "hard time") called me to tell me he had just moved into isolated, remote little (not to mention pretty much crime-free) East-end, Saskatchewan, the village nearest our home. This was more than surprising: Why not a city where he could lose himself and where there would be jobs? And how had he even heard of Eastend? He said that he had heard of me, although I was never clear how, and that he wanted me to write a book about his life. But when I did meet with him (our spouses were also present), he told me that he didn't read, although his wife did, and apparently, he hadn't finished school. I was even more baffled as to how he would have heard of me, as I am fairly sure that obscure Western writers living in backwaters are not a common subject of conversation in maximum security prisons.

Events were moving more than a little too fast for me. Up to the moment I decided I wanted to write a book about Alex's life and death and began asking questions, I had led the safest, most secure and ordinary life possible, so suddenly I was something beyond surprised, and just a little frightened. But I was stirred, too, as if I had just wakened from a long dream into a bright, fast-moving, risky world, and I was disoriented, hardly knew which way to turn. It amazed me how quickly a life could move from safe into dangerous waters; just like *that*, unintentionally, by accident. And I could see that backing off, forgetting the whole idea of the book, was an option that would return me to a safe shore, and I have never been brave, never been a boat-rocker by nature, so why did I not just walk away? Actually, I thought I had when I called in *the fifth estate*.

And I was remembering how, when we were young in the fifties, and despite the prostitution, the famous bootlegger, the famous bookie, we knew that Saskatoon was a safe little city. It was a safe city in a safer world—at least a safer North America. There had been only about ten murders in the city between its inception in 1883 and 1961, with many years between each of them, and those murders were mostly readily solved, if not obvious. (There were four in the fifties.) If Saskatoon was safe, so was the province, at a rate of something like 1.4 murders per 100,000 people (in a province of under a million population) and this into 1962, the year of Alex's death. Murder statistics before the early sixties are unreliable, and often not gathered in any comprehensive way, but nationwide, when Alex and I were still in high school, the figure was about one murder per 100,000 people. By 1962, with our population at eighteen million, the rate had jumped to 1.47, reflecting the large changes in Canadian society, but still a number that placed Canada in the lower levels of homicides in the world, and despite all the shouting about "getting tough on crime," it has stayed low ever since.

So pretty, bright Alex, by this time a hard-working professional woman, was killed one night absolutely out of the blue, and as the people of the city cast about for a reason for this, many concluded that Alex was not what she had appeared to be, that she must have been a *slut* or a *tease*, or otherwise to blame. There is a strain of ugliness in all this that did and does us no credit as a society: that we couldn't simply conclude that it was a random act of violence, that she had the misfortune to be in a place at a time that made her the victim, and that the only appropriate reaction was horror, pity, and grief. Instead, the assumption was that, as we used to say, *she got what was coming to her.*

The era had a lot to do with this. In the forties, during the war, women had gained a kind of valour. If they were not among the many who joined the services and went overseas, they were back home working at men's jobs, taking on men's responsibilities with the family, managing the household with severe shortages and ration books, and doing what was called "war work." Even the movies reflected this strength, flexibility, and steadfastness in forties heroines who had character and personal power, as well as jobs and sometimes even careers, and managed things with self-assurance, competence, and flair.

But once the men came home and the fifties hit, with the booming economy that didn't need women's work, and the move out to suburbia even for working class people, women lost their freedoms and were reduced to roles of strenuous propriety (signalled often by the ubiquitous white Peter Pan collar and white gloves).

Boys were encouraged very early on to be men. Girls were kept children, their sexuality under the tightest of control, for as long as parents and the rest of society could possibly manage. *"All I want is a party doll,"* the 1957 Buddy Knox hit song went, and in our full, "poodle" skirts held out with pink and white crinolines and our little black velvet ballet-slipper shoes with coloured, light-catching confetti sprinkled on the toes, we were happy to be party dolls.

But being a party doll, a cute young girl with a nice figure who asked no more than an evening of good clean fun, ending with a decorous kiss—while this appeared to be easy and natural, it was not. It had a definite flip side. Even at working class Tech, our parents had firm expectations about our behaviour, our high school society laid down its own rules too, if you weren't to be seen as having joined the ranks of girls with "bad reputations," and most boys were just as keen as you were to stay on the right side of convention. Girls such as Alex and me followed the rules, came home mostly when we were told to, and despite necking, never went one step further. The penalties for breaking the rules—if you got caught—were too severe.

"Getting caught," of course, meant getting pregnant. In a world where rape was never spoken of, and murder happened elsewhere, getting pregnant was too terrifying a prospect even to consider. Abortions were generally not to be had, and often marriage, for one reason or another, was not possible, and thus, many parents decided that you would have the baby in secrecy and give it away. We all knew of the large yellow-brick house across the street from City Hospital where unmarried pregnant girls were housed by the Salvation Army while they waited to give birth. It figured in our worst nightmares.

In the fifties sexual choices were limited: don't have intercourse or any kind of sexual relations; have intercourse but practise *coitus interruptus*; or settle for long, sweaty, frustrating, back-seat "petting" sessions. Most of us, in fifties Saskatoon, stuck to the latter. And that meant that some of us were raped. We call it "date rape" now, but in the fifties it didn't have a name, and it was commonplace—not perhaps, actual rape, although it is likely that there were many more rapes than were ever reported—but certainly it was the rare one of us who had never been on a date where we had to fight physically to keep our virginity. Getting thrown out of a boy's car, having to walk home, or going home bruised and crying, but with virginity intact—these things happened a lot.

It is no wonder that among the girls I knew, the ideal, although rarely attained, was to get your grade twelve diploma in June, and to marry (while not pregnant) your boyfriend in July or August. And then the babies would start to come, the "diaper curtain," as one of my old St. Mary's friends called it, would descend, and for the next ten or fifteen years—the remainder of your youth—you would be lost to everything but the children, the household, the wifely duties. It seems to me now that, even loving our children and our husbands, it was little more than slavery. It's no wonder that after 1968, when Canadian divorce laws began to allow for grounds of "marriage breakdown," a lot of these early marriages ended in divorce.

If I was determined, eventually, when a high school guidance counsellor and my art teacher showed me that even I might go to university, that I would do so and that I wouldn't leave until I had a degree, it was because, as a child in a family of five, I knew—as Alex did—what lay in store for me the moment I married. I wanted love in the form of a husband as much as my friends did, but I wanted middle-class respectability and a decent income just as much. And the only way

I could be sure I would get those things was to get them myself.

All of Alex's old friends insist that though she wanted to get married someday and to have children, there was no way she wanted to be one of those "graduate in June, marry in July" girls. She wanted to go interesting places and to do interesting things before she would even consider being tied down like that—up all night looking after sick ones, or nursing a new baby, and then on her feet all day, washing diapers and chasing toddlers, while she was still young, and the wide world was out there waiting for her. Locked into the fifties ethic, clear, at least, about what we didn't want, short of rape Alex and I were not the "kind of girls" who got pregnant out of wedlock.

There hadn't been a murder in Saskatoon through our entire childhoods, and it is no wonder that we felt safe, and no wonder that when pretty, smart, decent Alex met her brutal death, the city was stunned, shocked, and beyond horrified. Finding no handy culprit, it turned to Alex as the cause of her own death—she had to have been responsible, because otherwise there would be a lot more deaths in the city, and of pretty young women. And that turned into the rumours of promiscuity, of involvement in drug crime, of "pregnancy without benefit of husband," of affairs with married men, and of whatever other disreputable behaviour might lead to somebody wanting to kill you. In the minds of many people, unable to believe that a murderer was loose in our city, it had to have been her fault. I suppose it could even be said that if she had brought her murder on herself by her bad behaviour, then it could not be *our* fault—"our" being the citizens of our city.

But those of us who knew her, who had gone to school with her, whether we were close friends or not, knew better. Whatever had happened to her that night, not one of us would have believed she had done anything more to bring it on than to have gone alone to the weir, and to have stayed too long, until it was dark and everyone else had gone home. It seemed to me that Alex deserved better, much better, that we owed her, among other things, the restoration of her reputation, that phone taps and ex-convicts and the other unexplained and unpleasant things that might happen to me would be worth it, if we could all, finally, know the truth about what had happened that night.

I seemed to have committed myself to writing a book. It had never been that I didn't want to write one and was merely trying to avoid doing it, as much as that I couldn't grasp the true story. Alex's story was too brief, her life too brief, and the murder too sudden and disconnected from her life, or so it seemed to me then. And yet, already people were asking me if my book was finished, and when it would be published, and I was beginning to feel that I no longer had a choice, that so many people were depending on me to tell them Alex's story, that somehow, I would have to do it.

## Chapter Four
## Love Me Tender

That first day in September 1954, when I crossed the parking lot, passing between the arena and the Legion building, and then over the back alley to the Saskatoon Technical Collegiate, going up the stairs and in the side door that I would use every day for the next four years, I was nervous. But I'd walked the last few blocks to the school in a crowd of kids all going to the same place, and even though I knew none of them, and my stomach was queasy with anxiety, I was positively buoyant with excitement, because I'd made it to high school at last. That I was going to Tech, and not Nutana or Bedford Road Collegiate, caused me no concern. Tech was closest to where I lived. I knew no reason not to go there, as (I was overjoyed to know) my parents couldn't afford to send me to the convent where my best friends were headed, and surely there would be one or two kids from St. Mary's at Tech, and if not, well, I would get to know the people in my class. I wouldn't walk there by myself for very long, I was sure.

Sometime during my grade nine year our family moved across the river into Nutana. For reasons I cannot remember, I didn't change schools, but kept on trekking every day for the rest of that year and the next three, across the river toward downtown and working class Tech. I suppose I was afraid to change schools; I've never been fond of change. Two of my younger sisters went to Nutana Collegiate and I can't recall either of them ever complaining that they didn't feel they belonged at Nutana, though they came from a working class home. But I think my fear was that I wouldn't fit in.

Now I think with some anger of the purpose Tech was designed to serve: to keep us in our place, we kids of immigrants, the uneducated, the labouring class. We were to go to school to be trained to keep right on being the working class, while kids at Nutana understood that they were to go to university, to acquire professions, and eventually, to run the city and the province, maybe even the country. ("We are trained to be leaders," an eighteen-year-old told me recently, innocently, of the Toronto private school he was attending.)

Alex's situation was, in that regard, very different from mine. She was sent to the city to get a high school education while her parents stayed behind on the farm. But she had an older sister in town, Marie, the oldest of the four Wiwcharuk girls—Marie, Pearl, Ann, and Alex. Marie and her husband, as I mentioned earlier, ran a successful plumbing and heating business in the Exhibition District, where he and Marie and their children also lived. Farm families who were keen for their children to go to high school often sent them into the city if there was a family member with whom they could stay, because city high schools, often having better qualified teachers and more facilities for sports, the sciences, and sometimes even music and art, were seen as better than the country ones. It was also the fact that in the fifties, before school amalgamation and routine bussing of farm and rural kids to a consolidated school, going to high school too often meant having to board during the week in the nearest big town. If you were going to have to board out in any case, it only made sense, provided a proper, safe living situation could be found, to go on to the city.

Because Alex was sent to live with her sister, and that sister lived in the Exhibition District, a long bus ride away from Tech, it occurred to me now to wonder what she was doing at Tech at all, when Nutana was on the same side of the river, and so much closer. For some time I had been trying to track down a close high school friend of Alex's, but the only one—aside from the girl who lived on the same block as Alex's older sister, and who was very close to Alex—was someone who had been in her class at Tech. In answer to my question as to why Alex went to Tech and not Nutana, she told me that she and a number of other young Ukrainian girls had been sent to the city to go to high school and were staying together in a Ukrainian institute and dormitory. She said, "Our parents wanted us to get the best education there was, and that meant, in those days, going to Nutana Collegiate." (This imperative was very much in line with everything I knew about Ukrainian families, how ambitious they were for their children, what sacrifices they would make to be sure those children were educated into, at least, the middle class.) Nutana, though, did not accept them, so, however unexpectedly, Alex wound up spending four years at the Saskatoon Technical Collegiate Institute. (I would eventually hear the story from several of those eager Ukrainian farm girls of how they were turned away from Nutana for what certainly appeared to me to be spurious reasons.)

I needed to see what we had both looked like then, and to try to remember where our paths might have crossed, and if I hadn't yet found friends full of stories about Alex in high school, I had come up with another avenue. The next time I was in the city I went to the public library, asked the librarians to dig out the old *Techalogue*, our high school yearbook. *Tech Talk*, our school newspaper, was too much to ask for, I thought—since it was unbound, surely all copies of it had vanished years ago. I sat down for the first of what would be many times, pen in hand, notebook open before me, and began to comb the yearbooks from 1954 through 1958.

Our class pictures in the early grades were en masse; it was only in grade eleven and twelve that individual headshots were used, and full body shots only in group pictures such as the senior girls' volleyball team or the students' representative council, where we stood, frowning in the sunshine, on the school steps or lawn. Alex looked slim in the early years. It wasn't until grade eleven that she began, at least in her picture, to look a little plump, and I saw that in that same year I had also gained a disconcertingly large amount of weight. Something to do with hormones, I guessed, but I remember, too, how often high school bored me, how much I hated the "rules" we kids had generated ourselves to govern how we behaved and what we did (silly ones such as never wearing pink for fear of being called a "fairy"), and how much there was that I might have done to alleviate my boredom, but I refused, finding such things unthinkable. I think the eating was a result of that sheer boredom, and of the constraints that hedged us in at every turn—smart girls in a world where being smart wasn't worth that much. If boys had their societal crosses to bear, and they did, they weren't much compared to those that we girls had to deal with in the fifties.

The last firm memory I have of Alex took place in the gym where we had our dance practices and where we were sent to eat our lunches. I remember that my friends and I were the last to leave that day, and that Alex and a few of her girlfriends were already walking away, when one of my friends called something to her. Alex turned to look over her right shoulder to throw back a short, polite reply. I remember that she did not smile, that she seemed, if anything, bored, or perhaps even a little sad, and that she was wearing a wine-coloured cardigan over a white blouse, and a straight skirt in either navy or dark green that came well below her knees. I remember the rich colouring in her cheeks, the darkness of her thick, short hair, and especially, in that moment, her seriousness. I sometimes think that we had more maturity then, at seventeen—a result of our trained submissiveness—than we did a few years later when we had been more or less freed into the world and were acting out all the things forbidden us for so long. But why that picture of her, and that glance should be fixed in my mind for nearly fifty years, I do not know. What did I know that day that never came to consciousness? Did I know that, somehow, somewhere, one day we would be engaged together in an attempt to redeem her suffering and death, and perhaps even to find justice for her?

Thinking of that glance of Alex's that I thought bored or sad, I sensed that she, too, felt the constriction of our lives: *You must get an education*, and *Nice girls don't do that*, and *Do as you're told*, when we had naturally such an abundance, a veritable torrent of life-desiring energy raging through us, at sixteen, at seventeen, at eighteen. We were kept children far too long in those days, girls especially. I think that was the source of our boredom, that and a simmering but buried rage at the absurdity of our position, which we did not recognize intellectually, so well-governed were we, but which dragged at us well below the surface calm of our lives. We yearned for what we thought was freedom, although instead of true freedom, we yearned for love, for a husband, for our very own family, because that was all most of us knew; it was what our culture taught us.

My perusal of the yearbooks showed me that Alex, in fact, was even then recognizable as the beauty queen she would become. I wondered why I had remembered her all these years as unremarkable looking, and that I had been so surprised and dubious, on reading of her death, to hear that she had won beauty contests, enough so that for a second I wondered if the murdered girl could be someone other than the one I'd known. I studied that face again, and it seemed to me that it somehow lacked . . . *something*—some, for lack of a better word, *focus*, or a distillation of spirit that I now know comes, if it comes at all, later in life. Maybe it was just the state of being a teenager in the late fifties, before the late sixties when the world burst open. I looked vague and unformed myself, much more so, in fact, than Alex did. Alex's eyes were dark and strong-looking, serious eyes, I thought, and now I saw that her mouth was well-formed and beautiful.

I found myself gazing obsessively at her face, reading the class notes with close attention, as if they might reveal something more about her, even though I knew very well that those who wrote them had had to think long and hard to come up with something—anything—to say about their classmates, while giggling to each other about the impossibility of saying something *nice* about *that* person, but knowing that the teacher-adviser would not pass anything else. And nothing snide, either, would get past the adviser. The result was that the most innocuous person in class might wind up with the nicest note. At the end of our grade nine year, mine reads, *"The friendly kid who has such a charming personality,"* read *dork*, although in those days we would have said *pill*, with flippant contempt.

We—Alex and I—are both in the choir picture, but only she is in the cast picture for *The Pirates of Penzance*, that year's production, although I sang in it too, and will never forget the ghastly pale-yellow cotton pinafore things we wore.

Alex's class note reads, *"1G's favourite half-pint,"* which sounds marginally friendlier than my note. I was in 1I—we weren't in the same class at any time through our high school years, which is the main reason we were never close friends, and why I now studied her pictures and notes with such intensity, hoping some long-forgotten incident would suddenly tumble from its hiding place. In the choir picture, I stand near the girl who was my closest friend then, and both of us are close to Alex.

How serious we all were, a little frightened to find ourselves in high school, mixed in with what must have seemed to us hundreds of other kids just like us, most of whom we'd never even seen before, and the lower hall—the freshie hall—so crowded with kids at breaks that you could only walk down it by dodging and squeezing between bodies. Or maybe we were concerned about our choir leader whose temper I remember as being explosive. I had no recollection of why I joined choir, I was not a singer, but it was probably because I felt I had to do *something*, and the usual—sports—I had always avoided. I found, after I'd searched all four yearbooks, that in that respect I was like Alex: she was not in even one picture of a sports team.

But we were both in Drama Club that year. Alex is listed as being in a play called *Balcony Scene*, and she tied with another girl for "Best Actress" of the evening of plays—her play was chosen to represent our school in the city "playdowns." In her class picture, sitting next to her homeroom teacher, Miss Kerr, Alex is prim, and wearing saddle shoes and white socks. Part of our code was that the socks had to be brilliantly, spotlessly white, and to achieve this, to our mothers' despair (because it wore the socks out in no time), we would soak them in bleach.

Her class note reads, *"Always laughing, always gay, that's our Alex of 2CA."*

We are both in the grade eleven Drama Club picture too, where, once again, Alex was chosen as Best Actress of the evening's three plays. I remember sitting in the audience as the adjudicator spoke, and being startled by the choice. It was in the nature of a revelation for me; I thought, *Oh, so that is what acting is,* because I had not even noticed her when she said her lines. They simply registered and then I turned my attention to the next actor speaking, whom I'd recognized as acting. It was then that I realized that all overt sense of performing had to be buried. And the class notes for Alex's grade eleven year: *"You're nothing but a hound dog so don't be cruel; use 'Love Me Tender' as your rule. Listen to Elvis and don't be a fool."* I suspected that this probably was something the writers had collected from somewhere, and although it was devoid of any meaning, they liked the hipster feel of it and chose to use it on Alex because nothing more personally significant had come to mind. Remembering what high school was like, I am sure they were very pleased with themselves over that note. (It occurs to me to wonder how Alex would have explained it to her mother and father.)

In the grade twelve pictures Alex appears again with the Drama Club (where she is listed as club secretary) but she does not even place in the Best Actress listing. What a disappointment that must have been for her, her third year in Drama Club, and declared Best Actress twice, only to be ignored this time, when she might have expected it, when it might have mattered most to her. Her grade twelve class was 4C: *"Great in endeavour, small in*

*size. Shows enthusiasm in each enterprize.[sic] Ambition: Stewardess."*
(The joke here was the reference to the town she'd come from.)

Rock and roll was our music, and every Friday noon our gymnasium reverberated to its sounds while a couple of hundred teenagers twisted, stomped, and did that peculiar little hop-skip with the hip thrown out for a beat, arms extended, hands clasping the partner's hands, and then the spin, sometimes only the girl, sometimes both the girl and the boy. To be able to jive, to be good at it, to have your own style, that was what we aimed for. Every Friday noon hour for the four years Alex and I were students at Tech we went down to the gym and joined in the dancing to Elvis's "Blue Suede Shoes," or to Bill Haley's "Rock Around the Clock." Or rather, as things were in those days, if we were in grade nine we sat on the folding chairs that lined the walls, and at that, mostly at the back of the gym, the farthest from the stage, or else we stood in tightly packed clusters and unruly rows and giggled with our friends, moved our hips and feet to the music, and enviously—trying not to show our envy—watched the seniors dance.

By grade ten we'd moved up toward the centre of the gym—the grade nine and ten boys must have been leaning against the walls or standing in groups in the doorways, or maybe hadn't come at all—and sometimes danced with other girls, and once in a long while, an exceptionally pretty girl, or maybe one who had a steady boyfriend, would actually move front and centre and dance with a boy.

By grade eleven we were bolder, more sure of ourselves, knew most of our peers, and understood our own social system better, so we moved to the stage end of the gym, sat boldly on the chairs near to it, or stood, swaying and tapping our feet invitingly to the music so that boys might ask us to dance. The goal was to dance enough times not to be seen to be a wallflower, a fate worse than death by torture; it *was* death by torture. If we couldn't pull that off, we were better not coming to dance practice at all, and some people never did. But not me, and not Alex. We were in there, scared but eager, and by grade twelve, both of us without steady boyfriends, we still danced enough times not to be seen as unwanted and unlovely, as embarrassing pills.

We did not understand that this system was also torture for many of the boys. I can imagine how many girls spent that noon hour walking the riverbank with their girlfriends, their hearts and souls back in the gym with the rest of the school, but their minds steadfastly on something else—anything else—knowing that dance practice, for them, was only humiliation. Or how many boys got in their cars and drove elsewhere that noon hour, also wishing to be in the gym, a pretty girl spinning at their fingertips, but not daring to risk failure—expecting, as did so many girls, that absolute failure was likely to be their humiliating lot. It wasn't just the lot of those who were fat, or smelly, or whose nose always ran, or whose hair stuck out like a dust mop, or who appeared in clothes that were tattered and filthy, or worse, unfashionable, it was the lot of the ordinary in appearance, of the shy, of anyone who was perceived to be in any way different from the accepted standard. If we occasionally, privately, dreamt of a world where you were chosen to dance based on your inner loveliness and your interesting mind, we were a whole lot more likely to dream of a world in which we were pretty and *with it*, and had boys lining up just to talk to us. For many of us, it was our first experience of the real injustice of the world. The only escape from it, we thought, was growing up.

When it wasn't dance practice day, those of us who brought brown bag lunches—and if there wasn't choir practice or Drama Club or a Students' Representative Council meeting to attend, or if we weren't athletes—would go downtown. Our school was sandwiched between the South Saskatchewan River and a large parking lot, with the Canadian Legion building directly behind the school (it would be torn down in 2007), and at the other side of the lot, the Saskatoon Civic Arena, now torn down in favour of a high-rise residence for seniors. We crossed between the buildings and walked a block north on 2nd Avenue, and we were downtown. We would go in groups, mostly of girls, and we would walk for half an hour or so through the various downtown stores that sold women's clothing, Eaton's being the first, best, and largest. We rarely bought anything. We just wandered around, bored out of our minds, and looked at the clothes. Or else one of us would be buying a pair of shoes with six of us lined up behind her, watching and giving advice.

We were teenage girls, a fairly newly minted class of humanity, at the outer edge of the western pioneering society. We were among the first of the generations to be defined by our consumer interests, to have an industry of consumption aimed at us, to have our natural interests and desires, our psyches, plumbed by adults in order to sell to us. Together, we created the modern teenager as a separate category. Other factors were at work, of course: the move to the suburbs, the creation of the nuclear family, the need for people in suburbs to have cars, the post-war prosperity, and so on. What seemed to us fated, ordained, the way the world was, was actually a creation of larger forces.

All through our high school years, Friday night was movie night. Mostly, we went in gangs, depending on what the movie was, all girls, or, if it was a rock-and-roll movie, boys too. Movie theatres were packed in the fifties; if you were late you couldn't even get a seat. And everybody you knew was there, enthralled by the big screen, and by the big stars, chosen not for their ability as actors, no matter how gifted they might happen to be, but for their charisma, for the way the camera loved them. (It would appear now, also for their docility, as they were not so much human beings as well-paid commodities whose lives were controlled by their employers.)

Mostly, we went to the Capitol Theatre on 2nd Avenue, the city's main street, just a few blocks straight north of Tech. The Capitol was opened in optimistic and prosperous 1929, and was by far the fanciest of the six movie theatres then extant, with its decor identified variously as Spanish, Italianate, or Turkish, and with medieval-flavoured decorations, and a fake star-studded ceiling. High on its interior walls were false balconies with pillars and windows behind them, and a painted backdrop of trees and church towers. Regrettably, and despite loud protests by many citizens, in the eighties the Capitol was torn down. But its decor had signalled pretty clearly to all of us who entered it that we could leave behind our humdrum lives, that we were entering the world of dreams.

It is hard to conjure for the younger reader raised on television just how big an influence those movies were on our lives, just how deeply the things we saw there were imprinted on our teenage minds. I still remember the tight, wine-coloured satin dress Marilyn Monroe wore in *How to Marry a Millionaire*, and how adorable she was even to a fourteen- or fifteen-year-old girl—with that famed vulnerability of which she could neither rid herself nor hide, even as she embarrassed us half to death, and even as we were baffled and deeply dismayed by her. And yet, the temptation was there, the possibility of her as a way to be a woman was opened to us. We held it in abeyance—who knew what adulthood might bring?

But I do remember one girl who went to high school with Alex and me—another Ukrainian girl, as it happens—doing a young girl's version of Monroe at a party, solely to attract boys, and how well it worked. It wasn't a direct imitation, but a kind of putting-on of Monroe's innocent sexiness. I think I felt more sorry for the girl than anything, probably because at a more mature level (which I was able to find in myself when I wasn't so blinded by the movies), I knew that the performance came out of some real wounding, as it did with Monroe, as well as that the girl couldn't possibly still be a virgin like the rest of us, that the boys saw this too, and that that was why it worked for her so well. I suppose we were taken aback partly because we knew instinctively that this wasn't a healthy sexuality; it was not about husbands-and-babies, it was about daddy-and-his-little-girl, it was about desperation and an unfillable hollow of need.

Although occasionally some girl might imitate Monroe's walk, or her facial expressions, to make the rest of us laugh, I do not remember us even talking about Monroe other than in shocked phrases or half-sentences, without finding adverbs or adjectives, and sometimes without even nouns, to express our confused responses to her. It was that fifties virgin–whore dichotomy again and the reason Marilyn Monroe so confounded us all was the innocent, wide-eyed way in which she managed to be both at once. (Her tragedy, and it was a tragedy, should have been enough in itself to cause the second wave of feminism. She was so used by men.)

I remember being torn: on the one hand, I wanted a happy marriage and I wanted to behave in the way I was told I was supposed to, but on the other, I wanted glamour, I wanted an independent life. And when I mentally juxtaposed the two, aware of the impossibility of having both, instead of recognizing that it was wrong to expect women to be submissive in marriage and to give up any hint of independence or autonomy in favour of husband and children, and being shown no alternatives, I just thought—we all thought—that somehow it would all work out. Instead of concerning ourselves with the falseness of those movies, and the real message behind them, we concentrated on the gorgeous dresses, the glamorous sets, the shots of famous places we'd never seen but dreamt that one day we would.

From these films we took away several messages: that to marry wealth was a reasonable goal (although wealth plus love was the highest goal of all); that näiveté, genuine innocence, was endearing and proper in a woman (as was being a blonde), especially if one could manage to be sexy at the same time—this was the period when the term sexy came into popular use to describe a trait to be at once desired and deplored—or perhaps it was that näiveté in a woman was itself sexy. And also, that we should want to be married to a nice, high-performing man (if we couldn't find a rich one), that we should have children, and that we should aspire to a life of peace and domesticity in the suburbs—but that none of this would be easy to achieve, as men, generally speaking, did not know what was good for them, and had to be cajoled and drawn toward the right and best thing. This, usually, in the face of a glamorous, enthralling, "bad" woman. It was always clear which of these two we were supposed to *want* to be. In many of our favourite films, the story was about not much else but negotiations for the prize of the star's virginity.

That the world would soon break wide open, destroying these stereotypes virtually forever, freeing us, a small handful of North American women, wasn't something we could have imagined, so submerged were we in that world of fifties movies, and fifties television: *Leave It to Beaver, Life with Father, I Love Lucy*. In the meantime, most of us were conflicted about what we should want: caught between the natural desire to have lives of our own, and the equally natural desire to marry and have children.

That was how we spent our Friday nights—dreaming at the movies. Saturday nights were, in my memory, reserved for parties and dances, or better, for dancing. I didn't have a steady boyfriend and I wasn't very pretty so I did not go to dances, not even school dances, because to do so would have meant an evening of leaning embarrassingly against the wall. Mostly, those dances were attended by steady couples, or those—both boys and girls—who had at least a hope of dancing. Whether Alex and her friends ever went, I don't know, but when I asked them if Alex had dated in high school, they all said yes, but hesitantly, and not one of them could remember the name of one boy she'd gone out with. I suspect that her dating was kept to a minimum, this because, in return for her room and board, her job was to help her older sister with the housework and to babysit for her nieces and nephews. Besides that, every Ukrainian person I spoke to told me that Ukrainian parents were stern disciplinarians; it is—or was—part of the culture, and what children did and said, where they went and with whom, and at what time they returned, was closely monitored. Marie, Alex's older sister, had parental responsibility for Alex as long as Alex lived in her house, and she told me herself that she kept a close eye on Alex. This did not mean that Alex couldn't go out, but most likely that she could go out only on weekends, and had a strict curfew.

The year I turned sixteen was the happiest year of my teenager-hood. A half-dozen or more of us, both boys and girls, and mostly from our same class, but one or two from other classes, used to hold a dance party every Saturday night. boys would go round in somebody's car and pick us girls one and we would all go to somebody's house—we m home to home—and we would dance until mid-weren't dating each other and never did, and the boys seemed to feel responsible for us. They drank a moderate amount of beer, we drank Coke or water, and sometimes they would allow us a sip or two from their beer. I remember one girl getting too enthusiastic and the boy pulling the bottle away from her, and saying, sternly, "That's enough!"

We jived until we could barely stand up; every Saturday night I would lose five pounds (which, of course, I'd regain during the week). This went on even after I had a weekend job in Food Services at the university. I cannot believe now that I could be on my feet all day in the cafeteria cleaning tables, sweeping, making milkshakes, and then dance all night. As for drugs, marijuana was the only drug we had heard of then. Most of us didn't know what it was, much less how to get it, and if it had been available, we wouldn't have bothered, because what did you need drugs for when there was alcohol, and there was dancing?

But one night when the boys had picked us up, I remember that as we drove, they had a short, careful conversation, saying something like *How do you feel?* And a reply indicated nothing much was happening, and when we girls asked what they were talking about, they wouldn't tell us, and we didn't pursue it. You were careful with boys then, you didn't push them, you didn't demand. I remember thinking that some bad thing was entering our happiness, but I didn't quite know what it was, although I thought maybe it was that thing we'd heard about, but as I never asked in those years, and barely rem who those boys were, I can only guess that they ha their first taste of marijuana. That is the only men of drugs from the years 1954 to 1958.

As for Alex, a properly brought up and closely watched Ukrainian teenager, I think she must have yearned for freedom. Maybe that was what was behind that glance I saw her give that day nearly fifty years ago, in our last year of high school, and which, although I could not then understand it, I have never forgotten. A kind of weary patience, waiting for the time when she would be free.

## Chapter Five
## Wisdom

In June of 1958 we had reached the end of our childhoods. For many if not most of us at Tech, it was also the end of formal education. Our small gang of friends broke up, and while I still occasionally see a few of them, some I have never seen since, nor do I know what became of them. I stopped crossing the river every day, and began my five years of daily walking north along the river, but now on its east side, to what in those days seemed to be a kind of feudal estate high on the riverbank above and overlooking the river and downtown, and the old west side, to those beautiful warm pink-and-beige stone buildings, imitation Gothic, with their occasional crenellated tower and gargoyle under the eaves. I thought I had entered the kingdom of heaven. I thought that in one daring leap I had become one of the anointed.

I have always wanted to *know*; my desire to know began long ago, when I was a small child and the world seemed so incomprehensible and chaotic to me. This, because of our situation as a family, the mystery in the form of wilderness and wild animals, sky and winter hovering around us all the time, the precariousness of our existence there, the never knowing what the next year might bring, or where it might find us, and because of the struggle life was, and my parents not noticing their children needed explanations. And so, wanting nothing so much all my life (although I did not know that is what I wanted until I was old) as to learn what everything *meant*, at some level beyond conscious thought, I thought that there, at last, at university, I would learn the secrets of the universe. But my presence there was at best tenuous, I knew. I didn't want anybody to know that I didn't really belong there; I walked in fear all my first year, sure that I would be found out and expelled from the paradise of which I felt myself barely worthy. (And not knowing that half the student population, in from distant, hardscrabble farms and ranches and tiny villages, felt the same way, and was as determined as I to succeed.) And I gave barely a thought to high school and my friends there; I am sure that all that first year Alex's name and face never once crossed my mind. I had no idea what had become of her after graduation, and I don't remember wondering.

That fall, while I was shuffling happily down the campus sidewalks through the yellow, gold, and orange autumn leaves, and breathing in the crisp air mixed with the heady scent of the future, Alex had returned to her home country. She had gone to Yorkton, the city about an hour south of her home, in order to attend nursing school. In the fifties, girls were entering nursing in droves; it was one of the three professions routinely open to us: nursing, teaching, and secretarial work. Having been the first of her family to graduate from high school, she was now the first to go on to higher education. She had given no indication during high school that nursing was her plan, though. Twice in the school yearbooks she had recorded that her ambition was to be a stewardess, an ambition most of us wouldn't have dared to list even if we'd dreamt of such a thing. Stewardessing was a new profession, and it was viewed as very glamorous—you got to travel and see the world (imagine, a different city every night!), and to meet sophisticated, successful men—and not for the likes of the ordinary, as most of us felt ourselves to be.

I can actually remember reading Alex's class notes with friends, and our saying to each other, *"But she's too short!"* She was only five foot one, and in those days the rules governing who could qualify as a stewardess were strict: minimum height was five foot two. But you could also be too tall. You had to meet the airlines' standards of slimness too—some airlines actually weighed their stewardesses before a flight—and you had to be pretty. Presumably there was no scale or ruler to judge that, nor, I think, was this written anywhere as a requirement, but there was never any question about it. I'm sure this was because most passengers were men, not to mention that, of course, men run airlines, and how better to attract customers than the promise of gorgeous young women bending toward you and whispering, *"Coffee, tea, or milk?"* or, as the unfunny joke went, *"Coffee, tea, or me?"* (It is only in the last few years that prettiness seems to have stopped being mandatory, at least in Canada. I've been served by middle-aged, slightly overweight

women, much to my pleased astonishment, although I'm sure
some men would still rather be served by Miss Canada than by
somebody who reminds them of their mother.)

I'm sure we must have wondered, though not aloud,
whether Alex was pretty enough. The main reason we didn't
all give that "ambition" to the class notes editor was that to do
so would have been to declare we were pretty, and only the
very prettiest girls could get away with doing that, though most
wouldn't have because they knew that if they had, the other
girls would hate them. I can only think that by the time she
was seventeen and eighteen, both times she gave stewardessing
as her ambition, Alex must have begun to see herself as a pretty
girl. That must have meant that she was getting feedback from
her friends, her family, and maybe already from boys, that told
her she was growing into an attractive woman.

And yet, whenever I remembered her, I thought of her
as ordinary looking, and was surprised when others who had
known her in high school described her as "attractive." But
now, these many years later, when I studied her pictures in
our yearbooks, I could see the features that soon would earn
her the designation "beauty queen," and I wondered why
I hadn't noticed earlier. Maybe this was because we were
physically alike: I thought I was plain, and on my bad days,
worse than that, and maybe I simply believed that the same
was true of her.

We didn't see how discriminatory the airlines' rules were;
as if only the pretty could pour a cup of coffee, or hand out
a pillow. As if women existed only to please and serve men.

Rather than seeing the unfairness of it, we simply sighed, and accepted that we could never be stewardesses, and went elsewhere for jobs. It may also be that we saw the discrimination very well, but in a world where there were wallflowers and girls with "bad" reputations and a limited number of female professions, we believed ourselves to be helpless to do anything about it. Or else we knew at an unconscious level that the fight for fairness would cost us too much, and so we pretended to ourselves, as women do all over the world most of the time, that the unfairness didn't exist.

As a woman in her mid-seventies said to me when I was talking about the profession, she had wanted to be a stewardess herself when she was young, but—and here she paused for a moment, and then spoke too loudly, dropping her head in embarrassment, something happening in her throat, a near loss of control that would next be tears—"It was because you could *fly!*" After a second, she went on, her voice light now, matter-of-fact, though with a hint of irony, "When I was young, a girl couldn't be a pilot. So I thought, well, then I'll be a stewardess." It would take me weeks to sort out what I had heard: a sudden welling up of an old, still-powerful sorrow over a lost dream, mixed with the elder's self-deprecation of the foolishness of youth. I found myself responding with the writer's cold eye—*isn't that interesting!*—and at the same time, with the richest empathy. But until that moment, it hadn't occurred to me that lots of girls who became stewardesses really only wanted to fly, and regarded their work as what you had to do to get into the air.

This motive wouldn't have entered my head. Other than loving to dance, I was in no way physical, I hated sports; other than boys, paradise to me was a good book, and what I wanted most at that time in my life was a brilliant education. I wanted desperately to enter the heady realm of those who had read great literature, who could quote and recommend and understand, who could stride the world in the seven-league boots of knowledge. And I was fearful, very fearful—why else at that age to retreat into books? It wouldn't occur to me then to want to fly—that flying was the reason many girls might choose to be stewardesses.

Maybe I had misread Alex in this one important way: that she dreamt not of glamour, foreign lands, great cities, and handsome rich men, but of lifting herself above the mundane world; she dreamt of going higher, of soaring beyond the rooftops of her childhood village, and beyond the green pastures and dark forests of her own land, and even beyond the provincial little city of Saskatoon. *Flying* meant adventure, daring, escape from the chains of fifties girlhood.

Neither Alex nor I figured on what falling in love, provided the love was mutual, might do to our dreams. I married during the summer between my third and fourth year at university, on my twenty-first birthday. Unbelievably, I thought I was getting dangerously close to being an old maid. Shocking, when you think that today the average age of marriage for Canadian women is twenty-seven. I doubt that the prospect of spinsterhood worried pretty, popular, and confident Alex much. At twenty-three, she wasn't married or engaged to be married, and I am sure that this was only because she chose not to be.

There was one more requirement to be a stewardess: that you had to be a graduate nurse. No one close to Alex was able to tell me whether or not she had decided to go to nursing school with the purpose of eventually qualifying as a stewardess, but no one would rule it out as a motive either. She stuck with that ambition in our class notes for two years running, so I know she had to be serious about it.

I was being visited by a ghost. Not a white-sheet ghost going *woo-woo* and floating off the floor, arms outstretched, trying to scare me to death, but an experience that people, having no other name for it, call a ghost. One night, very late, and not being able to sleep, I was working in the basement at the computer, lost in whatever I was doing, and I saw, out of the corner of my eye, a white figure crouched against the far wall, crouched as though afraid—just a glimpse—and when I turned my head toward it, there was nothing and nobody there. The figure I thought I'd seen had been dressed in (or rather, was) some sort of white gown with hood and was very thin, but not tall, and the face—although I saw no face—was turned toward me. I dismissed what I'd seen as a fluke of light and shadow and went back to work. Some moments later, at the edge of my peripheral vision, I saw the same thing, only this time the figure was closer to me and still crouched in a fearful way, but when I looked, nothing. Again, thinking I'd imagined this, I returned to work.

Finally I saw the figure a third time, still crouched, and now closer yet to me. I came back to myself, my hands left the keys, and I thought, shivering a little, *What is going on here?* But when I turned my head and really looked, there was no figure, no person, not even a shadow. I was unnerved and anxious, and I shut down the computer and went back to bed. But I lay there for a long time, wondering who or what I had seen, or barely seen—or maybe I'd just imagined the whole thing—and although there was nothing identifiably Alex about the figure, I was sure it had been her.

What I left out of this account is the small black object, about a third the size of the figure, that was, in each tiny glimpse, placed between the white figure and me, and that was what the figure was afraid of. I don't even want to think what that was about, except to say that I wasn't in the least frightened by the figure—it was, if anything, pathetic. It was the angular black object that was causing me unease, and this was the reason I left the basement; it had seemed to me that Alex wanted to talk to me, wanted to approach me, but couldn't get any closer because of it. I see now that its blackness, its lack of features of any kind except that angularity of form, might well have been an absence—the absence of feeling, compassion, love, goodness. It was evil, I was sure, whatever it was.

The next time she came to me was months later. Again, it was night, and I was sound asleep beside my husband. But something disturbed my sleep, and I turned from one side, or was in the process of turning from one side to the other, when I groggily saw an erect, graceful white figure that seemed to be leaving our bedroom, as if it had been at our bedside and was now moving away, out the door, its back to me. Most surprising and lovely was the shining white cat—incandescent, large, full rather than sleek—that jumped off the covers over my feet, where it seemed to have been resting, to follow the white figure. And that was all. I was left this time with a feeling of awe, and of happiness that Alex had left behind or managed somehow to get rid of that black *thing* that dogged her, and was now accompanied by—well, what? For a long time, I couldn't figure out what that beautiful, weightless, white cat was, until one day, as I sat gazing out the window thinking about her, it came to me. It was, I decided, a guardian spirit; an angel, if you like.

That she had come again only strengthened my resolve to write this book no matter what happened to me; no matter what happened in the investigation; even if I had to self-publish. Oh, if only she would speak to me, I thought; if only she would tell me who it was that had taken her life. If only she could come to life again, and be Alex again, for all of us who care about her. Now I saw that the girl I'd barely known (although I wonder if I didn't know her better than I can remember), the one who for years at a time I never even thought of, had become dear to me, had taken over my heart. And she had done this, somehow, long after her death. If I could not recount one conversation with her, if I could not remember details, or knew who she had dated, or who her friends at school were, or what dress she had worn to grade twelve grad, I had come to know and love her anyway. It stuns me to think of how wide and deep the world is, and of what humans are capable if only they would open to that depth of world.

And I think, now that I am growing old, that this wisdom is part of what I sought nearly fifty years ago, when my heart's desire was to go to university, where I firmly believed the wisdom of the world was gathered, and where I would learn, at last, what wisdom was, what things meant. Although, I never conceived of this wisdom I dreamt of as being "what things meant." I thought it was facts, rules, insights and epigrams, equations and theorems, proposals and essays about . . . the turning of the wheels of the universe and time.

I begin to think now that it was not so much the identification and capture of her killer that she wanted, as never to be forgotten; she wanted her story told. To catch the murderer at last, well, that would be a bonus, and a much-desired one. Maybe, it occurred to me one day, Alex herself was the reason that Saskatoon remains constant to her memory; maybe she haunts the city, whispering in people's ears, floating through their dreams, touching them gently, and murmuring, *"Remember me, remember me."*

A year after they had decided to take on the case, in January 2004, *the fifth estate* aired its episode about Alex's life and death. They interwove commentary about the case, analysis of events and reports, and interviews with family members, witnesses, and those they had discovered as potential suspects, with a dramatic re-enactment of Alex's movements that night. They hired a young actor to play Alex, one whom all of us who had known Alex must have thought was nothing like her. She was, by the standards of the fifties, too thin, didn't appear to have Alex's feminine curves, and the coiffure she'd been given was wrong. Alex's essential womanliness was missing.

There was a mild furor in Saskatoon over that program; it served to bring back the original sense of horror and pity, and to remind Saskatoon people of things they remembered about that night or the event itself. I don't know how many calls the CBC received about it, but even I (having been interviewed on the episode) received a few, as well as a couple of letters. One of the letters was from Alex's sister, Ann, the closest to her in age, and in it she expressed her appreciation that Alex had not been forgotten, and pleasure at the recognition that family members were not the only ones who would never be able to rest easy until Alex had received justice. She offered to help me, too, with background about the family, and said that the rest of the family—or her sisters—were glad of what I was doing and would help me if they could.

Then one of the witnesses to Alex's last movements phoned. He'd been one of the boys looking longingly down at her from above as she sat alone gazing out across the river on the dam's apron in the hours before her disappearance. He said, with a deep regret, "Maybe if we'd gone down to talk to her then, we'd have kept away her killer." Another of the phone calls was from one of Alex's nieces, who talked to me about things of which I had had no previous knowledge, things that had happened to family members after Alex's death. Information was beginning to drop into my incompetent lap, some of it coming in ways so strange that I couldn't help but wonder if Alex, having acquired this inexperienced and cowardly biographer, wasn't up there in exasperation prodding people who knew things, with a long finger, to check in with me.

For example: a cousin of mine moved with his wife and family from the West Coast to Saskatoon. One night at a hockey game he happened to sit beside a woman who, they discovered in the course of their idle conversation, was daughter to another witness to Alex's disappearance. My cousin e-mailed me at once with the woman's name and phone number, and when the woman and I met for coffee, she handed me a typed account of what her father had told her he had seen that evening, before Alex reached the dam. I phoned him and he told me all about it himself. An old man now, he was still filled with anguish over what he thought he could have done that might have saved her, if only he hadn't been in such a hurry that night, if only he hadn't been late. Long after I forget every detail of his account, I will remember his decency, his anger, and his pain.

After the episode was aired people would come up to me on the street to tell me what they remembered about the time of Alex's disappearance and the finding of her body. At a public reading I was doing in Saskatoon, one woman told me about a certain man who had been bothering Alex, and another told me about a different man more or less in the same category. They told me what they could remember about these men, although this would turn out to be not that much, and in the end, it seems that neither of the men was responsible for Alex's death anyway. One of the people who talked to me after a reading told me about a family member who had had a bad experience in Saskatoon, before Alex's murder. It had happened at the end of the Second World War, when the girl in question was only ten years old.

She and two younger children were on a berry-picking expedition on the far side of the river from where, eighteen years later, Alex's body would be found, when a teenaged boy—described by her as "about sixteen"—rode up to them on a bike and lured her away. Safely out of sight of the others, he knocked her to the ground, beat her, tore her clothes from her, threatened her with a jackknife, and raped her, before she managed to escape from him. Then she wandered, dazed, bleeding, and still unclothed, toward the university campus, until a professor and his wife, out for a stroll, came upon her, covered her with the husband's jacket, and took her to the police station, and then to Saskatoon City Hospital, where she remained for several days. It turned out that her assailant returned to the other two children, both girls, ages eight and nine, but although he had told the first girl he was going to assault them, too, he did not, and he rode away on his bike across the CPR bridge—the one near which Alex's body would later be found—toward "the city."

I was able to find this awful story in the newspaper, and

I searched for word of capture of the rapist and, despite what seemed to be a good description of him and of the bike he was riding, did not find it. The family member who told me this story (a young child at the time) said that the boy who had committed this crime had not been caught, and that the family seemed to think that his father had been "someone important" and that was why the boy's identity was never divulged. She said that the person who had been assaulted (who remains, more than sixty years later, traumatized by that terrible assault not just on her person, but on her childhood, her very innocence) had always thought that because of the location and the nature of the violence that that same boy had been Alex's killer.

I suppose it is possible: if the boy had been sixteen at the time of this assault, he would have been only thirty-four when Alex was killed (seventy-eight today), and having demonstrated such a propensity for violence, and sexual violence, so young, he might well have gone on to murder. In fact, now that we know more about serial rapists and serial killers, he probably did. Because he was never identified, however, we may never know if he was also Alex's attacker. Because he was described in the newspaper as "rather poorly dressed," and riding a bike with rust on it—although he might well have stolen the bike—it seems unlikely he had an "important" father.

But such a conclusion by the members of that poor child's family serves also to demonstrate what happens when the police fail and then don't communicate sufficiently with the victim and the victim's family about their failure. I say this because this story—that the killer was known but a member of an "important" family—also became a rumour when they failed to capture Alex's killer. Whoever investigates this phenomenon—folklorists? sociologists? journalists?—could probably predict such a rumour as an outcome among the ordinary people of a place when vital information isn't given to them. Or, maybe even when it is. To hear, *We have failed*, or *We have so far failed*, will never satisfy some people, who will jump to the next conclusion: that the police know, but are *covering something up*.

Why didn't the *Star Phoenix* send up a hue and cry about the necessity of catching that boy? I suppose because in the forties we hadn't yet entered the era of truly mass media where a half-dozen reporters—this was Saskatoon—weren't there all vying with each other for the "scoop," swarming police officers and demanding or begging for information, sticking cameras in the child's parents' faces or the child's face, interviewing the neighbours, and family members, and writing thunderous editorials about the need to get tough on crime. There was no television news then, no television at all, the war was just ending, and people were focusing on that as the troops were beginning to come home. As well, the culture at that time was more inclined to accept authority than it is today. And so, as nearly as I could tell, within the month the story had disappeared from the newspaper, apparently never to be resurrected.

In the forties, the Saskatoon Police Service had only forty-plus officers to serve a city of between 43,000 and 46,000 people, virtually no modern equipment, and little training. I doubt today's police service would have failed in such a task, but in 1945, given these facts about the police force, trying to find that rapist must have seemed a Herculean task. They failed partly because they had little experience with such a crime. Most of the time in such cases, the victim would have been fifteen or older, perhaps a grown woman, and women (or the parents of teenage girls) would have preferred secrecy to what they would have to endure if they insisted on reporting the assault to the police. Thus, few would have been reported. But this was a child, and a traumatized and bleeding one, and the crime such an appalling one that her rescuers must have felt they had no choice, as responsible citizens and because her parents weren't there and couldn't for the moment be found, but to take her to the police station.

Perhaps all those Scottish Protestant policemen felt disgusted; perhaps they felt that this wasn't a case they cared to pursue, and that it would be better to send the girl home and not traumatize her further with their investigation; perhaps because the girl's father was a serviceman not yet demobilized there was no one with enough moral authority to fight for her. I can't help but think that because she was a child, and the event so terrible, and the times what they were, most people would think it better that she be taken home and told to forget it. In those days, there were a lot of things that women were told to go home and forget: the stillborn baby, the child given up for adoption or sent to an institution forever because it was not "normal," the rape, the beating by her husband.

I heard from others, after the episode aired, for example, about a friend who had been a university student and out with a few friends the night Alex disappeared. They'd been drinking beer, it was before midnight, and they pulled over at the bridge, parked the car, and went down the riverbank, out of sight, to relieve themselves. I'd been told that they'd heard something and had been questioned by the police, but when I got in touch with one of them and asked him, he replied that, yes, they had stopped by the bridge that night, but that he and his friends had seen and heard nothing and, no, they had never been questioned by the police. They just got back in the car and drove away and that was that.

People suggested to me that I should get in touch with so-and-so because so-and-so knew something. Sometimes the person had died; sometimes he was as far away as New York City, and sometimes he couldn't be found. None of these ever came to much. One story led me to spend a couple of afternoons at the library in Banff (I was there for a week at the Banff Centre for the Arts), reading microfilm of the *Banff Crag and Canyon* newspaper, where I could find no trace of the story I'd been told. Either the version I'd heard was too inaccurate to be recognizable in the newspaper accounts, or it had never happened at all, I thought, or it had happened all right, but not in or near Banff. Since the story involved death by misadventure, or a sort of unwilled suicide, and I found accounts of that sort of thing in the paper, although in the wrong time period, I felt sure that if it had happened as I'd been told, the paper would not have ignored it, and I should have been able to find it. And how I wished I had the time and the energy to do the same thing in Jasper, or Waterton Park, or even Waskesiu, until I found out what the true story was.

I read in the *Star Phoenix* that two weeks after Alex's body was found, a thirty-five-year-old electrician named Steve Kozaruk was found unconscious, from a combination of drugs and alcohol, in a Saskatoon hotel room in which also lay the body of an Aboriginal woman, Rose Whitehead, who had been strangled with a towel. Kozaruk went to prison for this crime, and, as might be expected, police were suspicious that he might also have been responsible for Alex's murder. But such a connection was never proven, and I don't recall seeing any suggestion in the newspaper at the time that this might be the case. Aside from Kozaruk, and the potential or real suspects mentioned by *the fifth estate*, of whom I'd previously known nothing, the community (and probably also the police) suspected several other identified and—eventually—incarcerated killers. Their names were Clifford Olson, David Threinen, Colin Thatcher, and Larry Fisher, all of them still alive today—three in prison, and one currently back at home on parole after having served his very long sentence. All of these four had gone to prison for crimes committed from seven to more than twenty years after Alex's death.

Alex died in the spring of 1962. Larry Fisher, the true killer in 1969 of Saskatoon nursing assistant Gail Miller (for whose rape and death David Milgaard was wrongly convicted and served twenty-three years in prison), would have been only about twelve years old and seems not to have been living in Saskatoon when Alex was killed. David Threinen, the abductor and killer of four Saskatoon children, was apprehended in 1975, having committed his crimes within the previous year or so. Speculation was that as Alex was small enough to be mistaken for a child, perhaps Threinen had been her killer. He would have been fourteen in 1962, and one of the phone calls I received from strangers concerned a story of a rape that the caller, who had known Threinen when they were both boys, alleged that he had committed in 1964.

Finally, in 1982 the most hateful of this hateful lot (if such comparisons can even be made), Clifford Olson, went to prison for the abduction and murder of eleven British Columbia children between the ages of nine and eighteen, murders which took place between November 1980 and his capture in August 1981. One source (*The Memory Box: One Hundred Years of Policing in Saskatoon, 1903–2003*) says that Olson was already in prison in Prince Albert, Saskatchewan, a small city north of Saskatoon, when Alex was killed in 1962, and so couldn't have done it, while another, earlier report (the *Star Phoenix*, in 1992) stated that he was released a month before her death and told prison officials he was going to Saskatoon. Although I still wonder about this, I have made no move to discover which story is correct. I leave that to the police, and am confident they know whether Olson was available or not, and perhaps have even questioned him about Alex's death, despite that long gap between her death and the deaths of the eleven children and young people for which he went to jail, and where he will remain for the rest of his life. Apparently, as is the case with most serial killers, he has bragged about many other murders he committed, but produced no proof of them.

A number of the people who phoned or spoke to me in person said that they had always believed that Colin Thatcher, who was convicted in 1984 of the murder of his former wife, also killed Alex. When I asked about this of people who had been involved in some way in Thatcher's trial, they assured me that when Thatcher was being tried for his wife's death, the police had followed this rumour and had concluded that it simply wasn't possible for him to have killed Alex. As for the "had always believed" part of the story that a few people insisted to me was the case, I think it unlikely. As far as I know, there was no reason at all why anybody in 1962 would have suspected Colin Thatcher, twenty-four years old at the time, and son of the leader of the opposition, soon to be provincial premier, as he had done nothing the public would have known about, other than being the son of "an important man," or "an important politician" (a story on which I will elaborate later), to cause anyone to suspect him then. I think that it was not until he was convicted twenty-two years later of a killing that surpassed even Alex's in sheer viciousness that people looked backward to Alex's death and tried to draw a link.

Eventually, I came to the decision that it was time to stop this fruitless trailing after rumours. There was no way I could ever solve the case; that had never been my purpose, as I kept reminding myself, and pursuing every one of these leads took a lot of time, time I could better use in writing my book. I began to have sympathy for the police, imagining how many of these "leads" they had chased down over the years, most likely to no avail. I began to see why they sometimes seemed uninterested or even a little bored or disgruntled when some citizen came in, breathless with excitement, to share "information." Or else, and I tried not to think this, I was circling the truth the whole time and just couldn't see it because I was missing some key piece to it all.

I also heard stories about Alex's body, awful stories, including that the tendons in her ankles had been cut to stop her from running, that there had been other mutilations, that there had been a certain man's ring found with her body, and so on. Some had told me that she carried a makeup kit, and others that her hair was in curlers. But as neither I nor *the fifth estate* had been allowed to see the autopsy report (nor had her family ever seen it—they weren't allowed to see it until 2005 or early 2006, forty-three or -four years after her death, when the office of the chief coroner finally released it, and I saw it too), no one knew what was true and what was rumour, or lies, or myth-making. But when I did see the autopsy report, there were metallic objects in or on the back of her skull which were identified as probably bobby pins, and when *the fifth estate*'s documentary showed the scene of all the material in Alex's file spread out over a laboratory table, a lipstick and a compact were there. If she had carried them to the weir, it seems that she indeed had had plans that night to meet someone before she went on to work. On the other hand, the television dramatization showed her making up her face in her own home before she left that night, and then walking away and leaving those items there, on her dressing table. Maybe the police had these items not because they were found at the crime scene but only to collect DNA from them.

When I had nearly completed the second version of this book, the one you are reading now, I began to realize that differences on the documentary tape from other versions of what had happened were not necessarily mistakes by the filmmakers, or a dramatizing of the facts for the sake of a good show, but were moments when the CBC producers knew more than I did, and despite talking with me fairly often as they did their research, they had not told me everything they knew, but had shown these things, without comment, in the documentary. When I finally realized that, I felt a moment of near-despair.

Before I'd begun even the first version of this book I had written a polite letter to the senior producer asking if I might have access to the program's files to aid my research, pointing out, among other things (such as that the CBC is a publicly funded operation), that without me, they'd have had no documentary. At first I received no reply, and I never did receive a reply from him in writing, not even by e-mail, but another staff member told me that he had said, simply, "*No!*" and that was that. When I complained, one of the other employees said that she would help me, but when I asked her, months later, for the answer to one question, she said that the material containing the answer was in the archives, but that she would have it brought up and would get back to me. I'm still waiting.

It would take me a long time to realize that in the segment in the television episode where police officers opened Alex's "file" (actually a large number of plastic-wrapped items spread out over a long table, as well as a mountain of paperwork filed in neat brown- or red-covered ring binders) and let the camera pan over them, there was only one item that—as far as I knew—hadn't previously been revealed to the public. That is, that the police, while appearing to be completely open, had carefully controlled the information, no one would even know that they had done so.

After *the fifth estate*'s episode was aired, and after the initial excitement died down a little, I kept working on my book and following leads, and so did the program's researchers. They were planning to do a follow-up program during the summer, when they hoped to have enough new information to point in the direction of Alex's killer, and these investigative journalists and researchers were, and are, not used to failure. I was every bit as hopeful as the other viewers of the program. With all the contacts I was receiving, and with what I had learned from *the fifth estate*, I was at last getting a look at what was known about the night Alex was murdered. It was fascinating, I was glad to have the information for the sake of my book, and for the sake of my own unsatisfied curiosity, but I was sure that none of it was details that the police wouldn't have—and thus, none of it would solve the crime.

Often, as I wandered across the hayfields, or across the prairie, alone, thinking about all of this, I would feel, hovering on the edge of my awareness, a sense of some great idea about life, that all of this—the people, the stories, the motives—was surely adding up to something, but that *something* wasn't who the killer was. I would see that glimmer of brightness again, that flash of colour and light and movement that was full of meaning, that was the piece of wisdom, or the key at last to all wisdom, that I had been searching for since I was a child. Try as I might, I could not bring it into focus.

Still, more than forty years after Alex's death, everybody I talked to, from law professors to strangers on the street, had a story to tell about what they knew, what they thought, what they remembered, what they suspected—had always suspected—and I was finding all of this material to be a mixture of facts and memories, rumours, theories, and sometimes, fantasy. It was so full of the humanity of the city—all those faces, those voices, those stories and ideas; the fact that people remembered and wanted to *know*, still wanted to know, as if to know would make it possible for them at last, in some way far bigger than the story itself, to rest easy—that I felt myself gasping for air, as it were, grasping for a string to pull me through all of this marvellous chaos, this beautiful richness that was life. Life along the South Saskatchewan River, in the city of Saskatoon, and the province of Saskatchewan.

Alex, dying too young, had invented nothing, done no courageous deeds, created no great works, and yet by the documentary of *the fifth estate* had become, more than forty years after her death, a national figure. I wondered if the girl who had come to me as a ghost, by all of this (for soon there would be my book, and surely, after that, a movie about her), still wanted the very fame that she had dreamt of attaining one day through her beauty and, perhaps—it suddenly occurred to me—her talent as an actress. It had all been stolen from her that night, all that glorious, exciting future, and she was determined, even from the other side of the grave, to have it anyway.

I knew myself to have developed into a singularly determined woman, this because I had never felt that I had any other choice in life if I was not to wind up desperately poor and living in some hopeless backwater. But I had never thought of Alex as also being a determined woman as well. I had seen her as a pretty, ambitionless young drifter, content to take life as it came, because until her death, life had been easy for her: first, as the youngest, most adored child, and then, as the prettiest girl in town, with everyone seeking her company. Now I was beginning to think that she had been as determined as I was, although she was set on a different future than the one I meant to have. And I marvelled at this idea too.

## Chapter Six
## Beauty

Although nobody I asked recalled Alex ever saying so, her friends seemed to think that wanting to be a stewardess might, indeed, have been her motive in applying for nursing school. Otherwise, it's hard for me to understand now why somebody like her, a girl eager for life and freedom, would have chosen to do nurses' training. Nursing students had to live in dormitories, and follow strict curfews and rules of conduct; nurses' training was a little like joining the army, so rigid was the hospital hierarchy, with doctors at the top of the medical staff, and student nurses and orderlies at the bottom, and a parallel structure in the non-medical with managers and staff at the top, and below them, ward clerks, kitchen and laundry staff, and cleaners. The nursing program was designed to keep the trainees children, not only through the requirement of living in a dorm and being in by ten on weekdays and eleven on weekends, but through the uniforms themselves, which signalled rank, and which also were designed to disguise the blossoming bodies of these young women, and which even hinted, sternly, of the nunnery.

Trainees wore caps simplified from the days of Florence Nightingale, and they were starched until they were stiff and pinned firmly to the back of the head. At City Hospital the uniform was a finely striped, girlish, pink-and-white full-skirted dress with a stiffly starched white bib apron worn over it, and with white cuffs and collars, like the cap, starched until they could stand alone. They must have been uncomfortable to wear, and were the height of impracticality as they were required to be pristine at all times, meaning endless washing, starching, and ironing by the hospital laundry. But not only were they a proud emblem of office, they acted also to establish a limit, a buffer zone, between nurse and patient. I can only think that this, too, had to have stemmed from the Florence Nightingale era when nursing was viewed as most improper work for young women.

There were attractions, however, for young Saskatchewan women to enter nursing training rather than university. Girls lived free in the dormitories, and their uniforms and other necessities were provided, while families of university students had to pay for their children's room and board, as well as for tuition, fees, and textbooks. A number of young women must have entered the nursing profession because their parents were anxious for them to have training "to fall back on," but couldn't afford to send them to secretarial school or to college, and this may have been one of the reasons that a girl as clever as Alex didn't acquire a university degree. Or else, bright as Alex was, and she was very bright indeed, academics was simply not where her interests lay.

Alex wouldn't have known it when she set off for Yorkton in the fall of 1958 to join her class of fifteen young nurses in training, but soon those Victorian dorms would be history. The reason that young women didn't have to pay tuition and got their room and board free was that the three-year program included, in the end, one full year of providing virtually free labour to the hospital where they trained. As one former nursing instructor in those days told me, a touch of the old anger still in her voice, "The hospital service component always had a way of taking precedence over the teaching component." But already, senior nurses were meeting with government health committees to begin a movement to take control of their own professional training.

Eventually, nursing training would be severed from hospitals, the program would become two years instead of three, and the dorms would be shut down. When Alex entered training she was part of the transition program where teaching was centralized, and for a three- to six-month period each year all the students would go to either Regina or Saskatoon to take classes, where they could devote themselves to their studies and not have to work in hospitals as well. I asked several nurses whether Alex and her class would have gone to Regina or Saskatoon—Yorkton is closer to Regina—but some said one, and some the other. In any case, her program was three years long, and aside from during the centralized teaching period, she was in Yorkton from the fall of 1958 into the summer of 1961.

Alex's second-oldest sister, Pearl, lived in Yorkton with her husband and children, and sometimes Alex and her girlfriends would stay overnight with them when they had stayed out too late and missed their curfew. More likely, though, they had all signed out to spend the night at Pearl's—whether Pearl knew this or not—because missing a curfew was a serious business, one that, if done too often, could get you sent home. (In the early fifties, when my mother caught those nurses sneaking in the window at the sanitarium long after curfew, all of the nursing and sanatarium hierarchy were involved in the disciplinary action.)

Alex would drop in to visit Pearl and her nieces and nephews sometimes by herself, and sometimes she also must have babysat for Pearl's children. During this period, after having become close to her older sister Ann—five years older—in the last years at home, before Ann left for good, and then close to her oldest sister, Marie—eighteen or so years older—during the four years of high school when Alex lived with her in Saskatoon, she now began to grow closer to Pearl. Alex's was a close-knit family, despite the ten children and the large differences in age between the oldest and Alex, the youngest, and it's clear that Alex was welcomed, protected, and loved by her big sisters, and probably also bossed by them, as they acted as stand-ins for her parents.

I found this dictum in the Yorkton nursing school's yearbook for 1960, when Alex was in her second year there:

> *Golden Rule for Nurses*
> *Do unto others as ye would*
> *That others do unto thy mother,*
> *Angels themselves can do no more.*

And yet, when she graduated, instead of applying to an air-
line—which nobody seems to have heard of her doing—Alex
took a job nursing, and so I am inclined to think that in the three
years after high school, the idea of stewardessing began to seem
less attractive. Perhaps that was because after going through the
very hard work that nursing training was in those days, she had
begun to value her profession for itself, and to want to practise it
not just when there was a plane crash, or when some business-
man had too much to drink and needed an aspirin. Maybe the
delight in being a beauty queen and the attentions of so many
young men had confused her. Or, maybe she had just been bid-
ing her time, trying to sort out all the imperatives we thought
we had no choice about, and to find what it was she really
wanted, how much she would risk, or dare.

In those years Alex blossomed into a very attractive young
woman, and men began to pursue her. Her family thinks that
she had no special boyfriend, but chose to go out in gangs of
girls and boys, but others remember her dating regularly. One
Yorkton man I talked to remembered going out on double
dates with Alex and her escort, and his girlfriend, who was also
a student nurse in Alex's class. He described Alex as "cuddly,"
a girl who thought nothing of hugging men she knew if she
ran into them on the street, or at a party, long before hugging
was the commonplace it is today. She was little, he told me, and
with a cute figure (having slimmed down by then), and men
flocked around her. After thinking for a moment, he added
that she was perhaps more naïve than the other girls. After
another pause, and with some emotion (common among the

men who had known her when telling me about her), he said, "I always thought of her as a precious little jewel."

Everybody describes her vivacity, her enthusiasm, and her general delight in being alive, and nearly everyone, both men and women, seems to have liked her, and enjoyed her company. One nurse, though, who had trained when Alex did, remarked to me that she always thought of Alex as one of those girls who "could do no wrong," meaning that she was recognized by everybody as something special and perhaps got away with things other girls couldn't have, that she was sometimes treated with special consideration. Not everyone shared that view. One of her nursing instructors, Alice Bittner, now retired but for many years supervisor of the operating rooms at the Yorkton hospital, who took the students on a three-month rotation there, recalled Alex as not standing out in any way as a student nurse, but as a pleasant, willing, quick, and hard-working "little girl."

Although I never did find one person who had disliked Alex—or, at least, would say so—one of the women who also grew up in Endeavour and graduated from the same nursing school a couple of years after Alex did, remarked, "Every class had one of those girls: very pretty, lots of boyfriends, always cheerful." She went on to say that she didn't think that Alex had had a lot of close girlfriends. "Other girls didn't want to get too close to a girl so pretty, one all the boys wanted to be with. She went out in a group; she was always cheerful and fun, but I don't believe she had any really close friends." Alex's 1960 yearbook class note reads,

*Alexandria is her name;*
*Being in by 10—what a shame*
*Grand little nurse she's going to be,*
*For she is our Queen you see.*

As if to underline the pleasant, good-spirited and capable young woman she undeniably was, in 1961 when she was still in training in Yorkton, the family's priest, Reverend B. Shwartz, published an article about her in the *Ukrainian Herald*, in which he praised her for being an exemplar of Ukrainian girlhood, in that she spoke the language, attended church faithfully, was making something of herself. Alex, he wrote, brought respect and honour to her parents and her family, and to Ukrainian society as a whole. It was perfectly true that Alex was all these things, but nonetheless it was a commonplace for Ukrainian girls to be fluent in Ukrainian and to be churchgoers in an age when most people went to church, and often, as members of the first Canadian-born generation, their families worked hard to be sure their children acquired an education. This article was written, I think, after she had been singled out as "special" by winning her first beauty contest. I can't help but suspect that the good priest, as with all the men who saw her, was charmed by that exceptionally pretty face.

It seems to me, though, a girl of the same time, that this must also have been, if only unconsciously, confusing to her: on the one hand, to be achieving independence at last and to be loving every second of it, to feel the world opening up to her, and on the other, to be celebrated as an exemplar of a severely traditional view of womanhood. Many girls of that period remember well this inner war.

I was only eighteen and nineteen when I went to work for five months each of two summers at the same hospital where Alex would start her career as a nurse. I was a summer-replacement ward clerk and I rotated for two days on each ward to fill in for people on vacation. This included, in my second summer, the operating room, a terrifying place with rituals I had no notion of, a place, I now think, I probably should never have been—not because I couldn't cope with the actual work I was supposed to be doing (although sometimes I couldn't) but because I was completely ignorant of simple medical matters that operating staff needed to know. I remember the day that a doctor had to take the phone from my hand—I was supposed to be booking surgeries—and say "gastroenteroscomy" for me because I'd never seen the word before.

On all the other wards it was my mundane task to deliver diet cards to each patient each day, which they would—if they were able—fill out and return to me. There were rules about what rooms I could enter with or without knocking, and what signs I could safely ignore, but once I walked in on an elderly man who was dying of bowel cancer, and a senior student nurse who was changing his dressings. When I pulled back the curtain surrounding his bed to slip through, I saw his pain, I saw the bloody, diseased abdomen, I saw the old man seeing my shock, and especially, the way he looked away from my appalled face with a kind of hopeless resignation, to stare at the ceiling. On another occasion I was told to deliver a message to a doctor who was in a room with a patient who had just suddenly, virtually inexplicably, died. I remember the doctor sitting in the nursing station with the chart open on his lap and saying plaintively, painfully, to no one, "But I just saw him; I was just here. As he stood with family by the bed, I couldn't stop myself from staring at my first dead human being.

And there was the day a four-year-old boy was brought in unconscious and alone, to the pediatric ward. All that long summer afternoon a senior intern on the other side of the glass sheet between the boy's crib and my chair and desk worked to save the child's life, as we gradually learned that he was a foster child, that he had eaten fertilizer left out on the lawn, and that a neighbour had found him and called an ambulance. The intern set up intravenous drips of mysterious substances, he discussed in muted tones what to do with staff who came round, he gave injections, he slapped the boy's face gently and called his name again and again; his anguish was controlled, but palpable. Hours later, the child never having regained consciousness, the intern gave up. The child was dead.

I saw other things: a woman recovering from a beating by her husband so bad that she didn't leave her bed for a week, a man to whom she would soon return, the nurses talking about her in hushed tones in the nursing station; the nurse who wore long-sleeved sweaters over her white uniform even in summer to hide the big black bruises on her arms; the doctor talking to the police on the phone in the ward office where I sat diligently putting blood pressures and temperatures into charts for a woman who had come in claiming she'd been raped, and him telling the police officer on the phone that she'd had "multiple" intercourse, the implication being that she was—probably—a prostitute. Apparently she was beneath consideration; she would get no help, sympathy, or justice.

I was merely a summer-replacement ward clerk, and I saw things I will never forget; I saw them when I was as young and green as anyone could possibly be, and I saw them without support or explanation. The things I saw changed me forever. How very much harder for young women such as Alex and her classmates, who would be the ones with their gloved hands inside that raw, bloody abdomen, who would be handing equipment to the senior resident, and cleaning the befouled bed afterwards, and for whom it would be mandatory not to show their fear or their horror. What a bizarre notion—that they were "little girls," that they had to be guarded and protected, kept virginal and under control, even as they were being taught to gain rigid control over their own instincts and emotions, including revulsion and compassion, even as they were companions to suffering and death.

I have said that I remembered Alex as a plain girl, and that others remember her as having a pleasant face, but that no one who went to high school with her would describe her during those days as a beauty, or saw any reason to expect that she would soon become one. But a beauty queen she definitely was. First, in 1960 she was chosen by her own Student Nurses' Associations to represent them in the Kinette's Ice Carnival in Yorkton. She won, and was named the Queen of the Ice Carnival. She was then picked by a local service club, who named her Yorkton Wheat Queen, to represent the city of Yorkton in the 1960 Saskatchewan Wheat Queen competition; there she was runner-up. Less than a year later, in 1961, after she had graduated from nursing and had returned to Saskatoon to live, her sister Marie and others, without telling her they had done so, entered her in a Saskatoon radio station's beauty competition being held to promote the upcoming concert by a not-yet-famous American country-and-western singer named Johnny Cash.

Alex was chosen to be his "Girl in Saskatoon," and in front of fifteen hundred people in the Saskatoon arena she was crowned, given an armful of long-stemmed red roses, and then she smiled up at Cash as he sang "The Girl in Saskatoon" to her. It was a humorous song, but in the newspaper photo of Alex holding her flowers and gazing, starry-eyed, up at him, it's apparent she hadn't noticed the silly chorus: "I'm freezin' but I'm burnin' for the girl in Saskatoon." (I am told that when Cash was informed that his pretty "Girl in Saskatoon" had been murdered, he never again sang that song.)

I know that I must have seen in the newspaper that Alex had been chosen to be Cash's "Girl in Saskatoon," but I have no memory of it. Maybe I ignored the account because by that time I cared only about jazz, or maybe I saw it but didn't recognize that pretty girl smiling up at Cash as someone I'd once known. Not having read the article, I wouldn't have known that Alex had moved back to the city, and anyway, my focus was the university campus, while hers was City Hospital. The wide river flowed between them; our paths would not have crossed.

I have wondered about this transformation of Alex's from ordinary-looking to beautiful, more than I have wondered about any other of the many unknowable details of her inner life. She was a short, dark, plump, pleasant, but essentially ordinary girl much like all the several hundred others of us in high school, and suddenly, only a year or two later, she was a girl so pretty she became the Yorkton Wheat Queen. Some of it is easy to see: she lost weight, and with her new, attractive body she grew more self-confident, more mature.

Her face and body were not the material of beauty queens of the period. Blondes were the movies' favourite, and Alex was dark—she had dark eyes, dark hair, and she lacked the greatly admired, pale complexion of the blonde. Her face (by this time) was heart-shaped, rather than the classic oval we'd all been taught was most beautiful, and although she had a small nose, a dainty chin, and an exquisitely shaped, full mouth, she lacked the perfect, unapproachable, willowy beauty of a Grace Kelly. The category Alex fell into was the same one that the queen-of-cute, Debbie Reynolds, belonged to, as did the very blonde, pretty, baby-faced Sandra Dee and Carol Lynley.

I think that her beauty-queen-calibre looks stemmed more from the rich colour in her face, from the brightness in her eyes, and from the glow of excitement and pleasure that she could not help giving off, than from any perfection of form, although that was present too. She hadn't expected any of this; she wasn't raised to this. She had been brought up to be decent, hard-working, and responsible, and not to assume that life owed her more. Her character shone through that pretty face, her surprise at such wonderful good fortune, and the hope that went with it for a dazzling future. This, rather than that overweening pride and self-awareness in their own good looks that you sometimes see in the faces of famous beauties as they pose, in a practised way, for the camera.

In a widely circulated newspaper photo of her sitting on the hood of a car, her left arm propping her into a sitting position, her left leg stretched out before her, her right leg bent at the knee, her gaze directed away from the camera—you can almost hear the photographer saying, "Good, now lift your chin, a little more, more—that's it!" before he snapped the shutter. Her right arm is extended straight from her shoulder and downward (she wears a wide bracelet on her wrist) so that her hand rests, fingers spread, on the shin of her right leg, and it is easy to see that the sophisticated wartime-pin-up pose designed to emphasize her slender waist and nicely shaped bosom was not one with which she was entirely comfortable. More sophisticated girls would have arched their backs provocatively, gazing not forward but up at the sky—or been persuaded to do so by a photographer—in order to emphasize their breasts. Not Alex; despite the pose, her back is straight, her feminine contours present but not flaunted.

Today the idea of beauty contests looks faintly embarrassing. They had been around since about 1906, the Miss America pageant since 1921 and the Miss Canada, a swimsuit competition, since 1946, but in the fifties they were tamed into decorous events. Every time you turned around, there was another one—Miss Wheat Queen, Miss City of (fill in the blank), Miss Campus Queen, Miss Ice Carnival Queen, Miss Hospitality Industry, Miss Indian Princess—each one beaming sweetly, a triumphant glitter in her eye, her tiara sparkling, her bouquet of American Beauty roses cradled in her arms the way it was assumed she would soon be cradling an infant.

Candace Savage, in her book *Beauty Queens: A Playful History*, says that young women entered beauty pageants as a way to "break open a life." That is, so much of the world was then closed off to girls; you could be a wife and mother, you could be a teacher, a nurse, or a secretary, you could clerk in a store, and the chances of living outside that tidy life laid out for you were, for most girls, few to none. But win a beauty contest and suddenly you were something special, you became a star, at least for a little while, you basked in attention, especially that of males, and often of powerful males, who saw you as a prize to be won, and who offered you opportunities you would not otherwise have had. You might even be noticed by the wider world, and find yourself in some exotic place doing exciting things. Or so the contestants hoped.

It seems to me that the very omnipresence of beauty queens and beauty competitions was a response to the prevailing cultural notions about women and their place in society. At some level, I think that this was a genuine effort to show proper reverence for the best in womanhood, an honouring of the idea of female purity, and a natural outgrowth of an age that, the rest of the time, did not much cherish the humanity and individuality of women. But the subtext was always pointing to the perfect "Moms" of television with their hair so well coiffed it looked shellacked, the chaste perfection of their attire, their unflappable calm, their wise love for their husbands and children, and especially, their complete willingness to sacrifice their own lives for them. Implicit in the "Miss Perfect Womanhood" of beauty competitions was the expectation of the marriage and children that would follow, not the science lab the winner would rule, or the law office she would command, the learned tomes she would write, or the art she would create.

I think, too, that beauty competitions were meant (also unconsciously) to replace the lack of real power of women, to offer them some modicum of it. Women might safely be allowed the power their beauty brought them because it was undeniable, an age-old female attribute that had always been cherished, honoured, and rewarded.

But, ultimately, beauty always is in the eye of the beholder; and among forty or fifty beautiful young women there was no sure way to choose who in purely physical terms was the most beautiful. It simply couldn't be done. Not to mention that Christian ethics, to which respect must be paid, made clear that physical beauty was worth nothing if the soul was not beautiful too. And how to measure the worth of the soul? By asking silly, unanswerable questions of the contestants, by turning a beauty pageant at least partially into a popularity contest, by looking at the quality of the lives the young women claimed to be leading outside the world of the pageant? It is no wonder that before long young women entered beauty contests not as mere ego-fulfillment, but in a calculating way, and while playing the role the pageant organizers required of them, fixed their eyes on the future to which the prizes and the measure of fame might more quickly bring them.

By 1961 Alex had been a beauty queen three times. Even if she didn't suffer from excessive vanity, she must by then have begun to think of herself as someone special, as someone who had been singled out by life for the best it had to offer. Alex must have come to see herself as a rare flower, and her expectations would have begun to blossom.

The combination of Alex's good looks and her sheer happiness and innocence were genuine, and everybody who gazed at pictures of her face on the day that her body was found saw that. Saskatoonians who didn't know her responded to that eagerness and sweetness, and it broke their hearts when they thought of her terrible death. It wasn't just the fact of its being too early, nor of her small place in the city's history as the victim of the first murder of its kind, nor even of the unspeakable way she died, in pain and terror, screaming and fighting to live, that made her death unforgettable. It was also that the killer had obliterated the innocent happiness that people saw shining in her face; in his fury he had obliterated her goodness and innocence. People knew that only pure evil could do such a thing, that that was why he had done it: because evil always wants to—has always wanted to—destroy innocence.

Alex, only by virtue of her beauty, had gained a measure of fame, and without meaning to, she radiated the aura of someone raised by the gods above the common herd.

In 1959 Alex's parents celebrated their fortieth wedding anniversary at a Yorkton hall their children rented for the occasion. It was the last time the entire family would be together. By the following year, 1960, when Alex would still have been training and enjoying her life in Yorkton, her parents had sold the farm where they had raised their children, and from which each day for eight years Alex had trudged the two miles to Bear School and two miles back again. They moved to an acreage a couple of miles south of Saskatoon. By that time, her father would have been in his mid-seventies and her mother near that age. After that, in the last year of her training, Alex occasionally would travel the 125 miles from Yorkton to visit her parents near Saskatoon. But after graduation in June 1961, she was hired to work as a nurse at Saskatoon City Hospital, to begin in mid-September, and once again, she would live close to her parents.

The summer of 1961 was a devastating drought year. June was the hottest and driest month ever recorded in western Canada, with an average yield of only 8.5 bushels to the acre. The Wiwcharuks had picked a good time to leave farming. At that time in our history, if farmers in Saskatchewan were doing poorly, the entire province felt it; the whole economy would be affected, and a kind of depression would fall over the countryside, and be felt in the cities too. Only children, able to run in paddling pools in backyards or to spend the long, hot days at public swimming pools in Saskatoon, as well as teenagers whose most serious interest in life was getting a tan, enjoyed the unrelenting heat. If Alex was fortunate in having older siblings who loved her and took care of her, she was lucky, too, in being able to spend much of that baking summer at Marie's cottage at Emma Lake, helping her with the children and the housework when she wasn't suntanning or swimming.

It is strange that when she was hired for her first job as a professional nurse at Saskatoon City Hospital, although she had graduated the previous spring, she didn't have the designation Registered Nurse, or simply R.N., as did her three roommates, all of whom had graduated with her. They would tell the coroner's jury that Alex was studying for her exams at the time of her death, but it is strange that she was the only one of them not to have acquired those precious initials. She was bright and fully capable of passing her exams if she studied, and the fact that she hadn't earned the R.N. makes me wonder just how committed to nursing she ultimately was. Clearly, Alex knew her future did not depend on being able to write those two letters after her name. Or maybe already nursing was palling for her and she was dreaming of something else. Or maybe she simply planned to study and to write—and pass—those difficult exams the very next time there was a sitting.

We all viewed our graduation day from our professional training with both great relief and some trepidation that we might have a hard time measuring up in the real world. But we knew, as Alex too must have, that childhood was behind us forever; we would soon be working as professionals with heavy responsibilities, and living, in Alex's case, for the first time in her life, not with her family, or in a carefully monitored, rule-governed situation but in whatever way she chose and could afford. It looked to all of us, as it must have to Alex, that the world was finally becoming available to us, and that we would have many, many years ahead in which to live out the unknown but satisfying futures we were beginning to make real.

Freedom meant, to us, having our own money and a small apartment, staying out as late as we felt like, maybe even all night, and for some of us, finally, because there was no longer anyone watching our every move, daring to sleep with our boyfriends. When we were in grade twelve the assumption among us was that a girl was still a virgin—except for those few who had "reputations"—and the very few who had proven they were not by becoming pregnant and dropping out of school before they were expelled as "bad influences" on the rest of us. Otherwise, we left high school as virgins. After that, once we were out of our teens, and certainly by the time we were twenty-three, as Alex was at her death, most of us were not. By then, even the most carefully brought up of us, at twenty-three, if we were not married, had become sexually experienced. Not necessarily greatly experienced, but having shaken off the guilt our earlier lives had instilled in us, we had willingly, in some cases even eagerly, given up our virginity.

As to whether Alex was a virgin or not at her death, I found it borderline impossible to even ask the question of people who loved and admired her, and in any case, those who might know, still heavily invested in that fifties mentality which said that a sexually active, unmarried woman is a defiled and shamed woman, would never tell me. Besides, a woman murdered as young as Alex was, forever after, could not be seen as anything but "pure." And so I didn't ask, and not having access to the material in the files of the Saskatoon Police Service, I couldn't find boyfriends to ask, and I couldn't find out what rumours, scurrilous or otherwise, the police had tracked down to their sources.

By 1960 the first contraceptive pill, Enovid, was in use in the United States. By 1961 Canada had approved it for use across the country, but only for therapeutic purposes (birth control was illegal here until 1969). But sometimes young nurses were asked to participate in drug trials, and who knows but that Alex might have been a part of one of them, and if she had access to contraceptives, the old fear of pregnancy that kept many a girl a virgin would have been alleviated. I wanted to know if she was a virgin or not, because I wanted to build a complete picture of her, I wanted to explore her psyche, to see her as one of us, and yet, because of her beauty, as in a different class. With apologies to those who loved her deeply, and looking only at the probabilities, I suspect that by then she was not. And yet, the possibility remains that even in 1961 when Johnny Cash was singing to her, even in 1962, even at twenty-three when the killer attacked her and raped her, that until that terrible moment, she was a virgin.

By August 1961, within a few weeks of Alex moving back to Saskatoon and beginning her first job as a nurse, I was about to start my fourth year of university and had just been married. My husband and I were both students and therefore poor, and by the spring of 1962 we'd moved from a tiny rented basement apartment on Saskatoon's east side, across the river again and into a slum apartment above a hardware store on the corner of 20th Street and Avenue A (its name was soon changed to Idylwyld Avenue and the hardware store torn down). Much to my surprise, eight years after leaving it—I had hoped forever—I was back living in what seemed an unchanged Riversdale on Saskatoon's working class west side.

The city itself had changed a great deal, though. According to the federal census, its population was now almost 96,000, although in 1960 the *Star Phoenix* had already declared it to be 100,000. Our new University Hospital, the third hospital in the city and by far the largest and most prestigious (one day to be called "Royal"), had finally opened its doors, as had a new city hall, and our first shopping centre out on Taylor Street at Clarence Avenue. When I began university in the fall of 1958 (and Alex left Saskatoon for nursing school in Yorkton), there were only about three thousand full-time students at the university; by 1962 there were six thousand, and new buildings—*sans* crenellated towers and gargoyles, but still built of that beautiful fieldstone—were popping up all over the campus.

Saskatoon still had a low crime rate, people were still not afraid to go out at night, parents did not worry about their children playing unsupervised on the streets and boulevards, and driving them to school to keep them safe rarely occurred; parents did not routinely lie awake nights worrying until their teenagers, off at some party or dance or movie, returned. (Or if they did, it was not that a gang or a mugger might accost them.) People often remarked to each other what a great place to raise children Saskatoon was then—big enough to provide good schools and cultural opportunities, but small enough to be affordable, safe, and cosy for its residents.

As well, Saskatoon's homicide statistics were hardly alarming. As I've said, there had been no murders in the forties, only four in the fifties, and in the year of Alex's death there would be only one other. Province-wide, the story was the same. In 1961 there had been fourteen murders, and in the year of Alex's death, thirteen. The country as a whole had low murder rates. In 1953 the Canadian population was only fourteen million, and there were 149 murders nationwide, making Canada generally a safe place to live. In 1961 there were 125, and in 1962, with John Diefenbaker from Prince Albert, Saskatchewan, in his last year as prime minister and a nationwide population of eighteen million, there were 265 murders, an increase of forty percent, but one typical of all Western nations, and one that would soon be followed by a drop that has held steady ever since.

By the early sixties, Saskatoon's character began to change in other ways, most noticeably as a result of the federal government's expanding immigration program (in response to a new climate that would not allow racial and ethnic discrimination) which brought people from African nations, the West Indies, and Southeast Asia into its ethnic and racial composition. This was the period, too, when First Nations families began to move into Saskatchewan's cities because of the desperate poverty on the Reserves. (University of Saskatchewan historian Bill Waiser suggests that as farms began to mechanize, there was less need for farm labour, work which many First Nations men had done.) Eventually, those small houses that my friends from St. Mary's School and Tech and I had lived in, and where people like Roy Romanow and Bill Davenport had been raised, would be occupied by First Nations families. Slowly, they would take their place on the lowest rung of the social ladder, and racism, once directed at Ukrainians and other Slavs, Asians and the first Black farmers, would now be aimed at them.

Some new freedom for women was in the air; discontent with the wide range of discriminatory practices and policies against women and with the sexual double standard was about to come to a head, and the behind-the-scenes work of the forties and fifties that would lead to the so-called sexual revolution was completed.

In the world of science, perhaps most relevant of all to Alex's life and death, only months after her murder, Watson, Wilkins, and Crick were awarded the Nobel Prize for their long work culminating in the determination of the molecular structure of DNA, a discovery that would usher in the possibility of cloning human beings, of world-shattering new medical possibilities, and that, ironically, might make it possible one day to identify Alex's killer.

We know it now as a pivotal moment in North American history, the moment when the foundations of the civil rights movement, the environmental movement, the hippie era, the era of the hydrogen bomb, the space age and other technological innovations including the personal computer, the genetic revolution, and, of course, the women's movement, were laid. That period remains so clear in my mind that it is hard for me to believe that people who today are middle-aged were either not alive then or were toddlers, and view the early sixties as the Dark Ages. I still remember clearly my sense of having emerged from the shadow of pioneer times to claim our places in a new, exciting, and wider modern world. In my memory of 1961 and 1962, the sun was always shining, and we were all very busy, doing interesting things, moving forward, we thought, from that tremulous and dark beginning, to a future that seemed boundless and unquestionably connected to the great world beyond our province's borders.

That was the summer I worked as office help for the Saskatoon Construction Association, then located on Duchess Street within a few blocks of Mead's Drugstore and Alex's suite. She could easily have been walking south on 7th Avenue to go to her job at the hospital on Queen Street as I was walking north two blocks over on 5th Avenue to my job, or perhaps we'd walked in the same direction at the same time but separated by two city blocks, and had no idea of our proximity. I didn't venture beyond the office into that area where she lived. I can imagine that I might have strolled over to Mead's once or twice during my lunch hour on some errand, but when my day was done, I headed as fast as possible in the opposite direction back to the apartment, my new husband, and my new life. Alex's path and mine never crossed.

She disappeared on May 18, 1962. While her family and her friends were searching frantically for her on the 19th, the unforgettable Marilyn Monroe was singing her famously seductive "Happy Birthday" to President Kennedy. By August, Marilyn, too, would be dead, the world, while offering certain undeniable benefits to pretty women, being also very hard on them. I was living in that seedy little apartment on the west side on June 1, 1962, when, having already read with only mild interest of Alex's disappearance, and with a great deal more interest of Monroe's version of "Happy Birthday," I opened the newspaper that morning and read that the night before, Alexandra Wiwcharuk's raped, battered body had been found.

I looked at the newspaper pictures uncomprehendingly, filled with something deeper than mere astonishment. Alex, that quiet, pretty, small Ukrainian girl from high school, and before that, from a pioneer farm on the edge of wilderness, had metamorphosed into a professional woman and a beauty queen, surprising enough in themselves, and now, she had been killed—suddenly, shockingly—killed. *Murdered.*

Staring at her picture in horror, the people of Saskatoon must have seen in Alex's glowing face their daughters, their sisters, their beloved ones. Perhaps, too, what they saw was themselves when they were just twenty-three, full of eagerness and excitement. No wonder citizens took her death so personally, no wonder pity rose from that deepest well of unnamed desire and love, of true humanity unsullied by the baseness of scurrilous rumours. No wonder none of us has ever been able to forget.

## Chapter Seven
## Spring

Friday, May 18, 1962, the first day of the Victoria Day long weekend, and the warmest day so far since the previous summer, reaching nearly 26 degrees Celsius. The whole city was giddy with it, those from warmer climates not able to conceive of the pleasure northerners feel when spring finally comes: the loosening of muscles held tight against the onslaught of winter, the lifting of the heart at the thought of the long, heat-delirious months ahead; ice gone from the river, bulky winter clothes put away, replaced with short-sleeved blouses and cool, full cotton skirts, so light against the legs after the heavy wool ones of winter, and sheepskin-lined, clumsy leather boots kicked off for the airy freedom of sandals.

The arrival of spring changes the timbre of an entire city. As dusk comes, everyone is outside, sitting on front steps, or walking down the sidewalks at a leisurely pace, smiling at any-one who passes by, children racing their bikes or tricycles, shrieking with sheer joy at the feel of the balmy spring air, young men in cars cruising street after street, windows rolled down, arms resting on the frame, circling and circling, looking for girls, and girls out in twos and threes, strolling the sidewalks gritty with the residue of melted snowbanks, swinging their skirts, and bending and moving their lithe torsos as if they can barely restrain themselves from breaking into dance, and full of hope for the company of boys. Beyond the sheer animal delight of the children, or the world-weary, contented pleasure of their elders, all things are alert now, the very air infused with the promise of adventure, romance, love.

And Alex, who turned twenty-three barely a month before, stuck in the city, having to work, the graveyard shift at that. All the delicious spring weekend would happen while she was locked in the hospital or sound asleep in the base-ment apartment she shared with three other young nurses. She had wanted to go to her sister Marie's "camp" at Emma Lake, and she had had other offers from young men, but had to refuse them all. Out now, on the half-pretext half-necessity of buying stamps and mailing two newly written letters at the drugstore less than a block away, she completes her errand but is reluctant to simply turn again and go home. She is eager to catch the couple of hours of spring left to her before she has to change into her stiff nursing uniform and her ugly white duty shoes, and hurry the seven blocks down 7th Avenue to Saskatoon City Hospital.

No one had seen her leave the apartment—Alice across the street looking for another apartment, Pauline working the evening shift at the hospital, Doreen out with friends—but Alex had mentioned to Doreen at least that she would go out to mail her letters, and maybe for a short stroll. Alice had even wondered if maybe she was meeting someone, because Alex had borrowed a blouse of hers to wear—odd if you were only going for a stroll before you had to go to work. But Alex must have thought the multicoloured blouse looked good with her bright green pants and her dark green cardigan. Doreen said that Alex was in the apartment sitting under the hair dryer when she returned briefly at about 8:30, while Alice said that when she came back downstairs from visiting their landlady at about 8:40, Alex was gone. The third roommate, Pauline, was working the evening shift, had been gone since three in the afternoon, and didn't return to the apartment until about midnight.

The pharmacy apprentice in the drugstore at the corner of 7th Avenue and 33rd Street, where Alex bought the stamps, remembered seeing her at 8:00 or 8:30. He said he remembered partly because of the "unusual and striking green outfit" she'd been wearing, and the joke—"pun," he said—they'd shared, but the store was full of customers and he didn't notice if she was alone or not. Nor did he ever tell the coroner's jury what the pun was. In any case, he also said that "she seemed to be in a happy mood," a state hardly unusual for Alex.

A busy young husband and father, driving to his home across the river after staying late at work to finish some paperwork, remembered seeing her after she'd mailed her letters and was walking along 33rd Street toward the river (on the south or railway embankment side where there was no sidewalk, only a narrow trail in the grass), with a tall, "well-built" man with "darkish" hair who, surprisingly for that time and place, was wearing a white shirt and a brown suit. Alex, her hands in the pockets of her green slacks (later, the man who saw her would describe them as "lime" green), was strolling along beside him, kicking her legs out in a casual, childlike, he thought "flirtatious" way. He remembered, too, when the man and Alex stopped for a moment about a half-block from Spadina Crescent, and stood facing each other, the dark tan on the man's neck and on the backs of his hands as he gestured. Alex seemed to be smiling up at him in a playful way, but the tall man had his back to the driver of the car, so his face wasn't visible.

Benign as it appeared, the scene nevertheless made the young husband uneasy, although he was never able to say exactly why, so his impulse had been to drive around the block and pass them again just to make sure the girl was all right. But he was late and hurrying, his wife was waiting, and you couldn't just drive around the block in any direction at that particular location—the high railway embankment on one side of 33rd Street allowed crossings only way back at Mead's Drugstore, and the streets were laid out too awkwardly (with extra-long blocks) on the other side of 33rd to make a rapid transit around the block, and straight ahead was the river.

But as he would later say, "Who would be wearing a suit there and then?" Eight-thirty or so in the evening of the beginning of the May long weekend, and by the river where people went for the pleasure of it, suggesting that the man had come from elsewhere, and was on his way elsewhere, possibly had stopped there just to meet Alex, or, on his way, had run into her. The young family man always said that his impression was that the brown-suited, tall man was trying to persuade Alex of something. But Alex was clearly not saying, *No, go away, leave me alone*; she was flirting, charmed by him and charming to him in her girlish way, and he could hardly have been a stranger to her. But no one, other than possibly the police, knows to this day who he was, or whether she saw him again that night.

Whoever he was, whatever happened between them, Alex then walked on alone under the CPR bridge, on the short distance to where the apron of the dam began—actually a weir, but everyone called it casually "the dam"—where, with the CPR bridge to her left and the weir to her right, she stepped over the fence that consisted of a rope attached loosely to low posts, and walked carefully onto the concrete apron that ran from that barrier down to the water, and from the weir itself and fish ladder, to within about five hundred feet of the bridge. Partway down the apron she sat down, pulled her knees up to her chin, wrapped her arms around them, and sat quietly, by herself, looking out over the swift-flowing river. By then dusk had come, it was growing late, it was perhaps nine o'clock, and she had to be at the hospital for her 11:30 p.m. shift.

She had positioned herself in a prominent place where she would easily be seen. Anyone seeing her there might have thought that she was waiting for someone and wanted to be sure that he (surely it was a he) would find her. And that she was so pretty a girl and alone must have appeared to others—men—whether it was meant that way or not, as an invitation to approach her. In 1962 in Saskatoon, no one would think this a dangerous thing for a young woman to do. The weir was a public place, on the edge of a busy road, and should have provided enough security.

Or perhaps Alex's sitting there by herself, conscious of her own good looks, aware that everyone could see her, was a sign of a young woman with a certain self-regard, sure in the admiration of whoever might be looking her way, with the innocent disbelief of the well-loved, well-protected child that anything bad could ever happen to her. Or perhaps she sat there with no other motives at all except to feel the spring air on her body, to watch the soothing, yet mysterious passage of the river, with the moonlight beginning to shine on it, and young and restless with spring, maybe she was imagining another life, led elsewhere.

And so she sat there, alone, gazing out over the swiftly flowing green water.

The boy who was fishing at the weir noticed her but, concentrating on his fishing, paid her no further attention, although he did say afterwards that there had been somebody else sitting on the concrete, too, but off to Alex's left, closer to the bridge. Besides that shadowy figure, above and behind her, standing at the rope-and-post barrier, were two fifteen-year-old boys. They were watching her, the bolder one urging the other to go down with him and talk to Alex, the shyer of them resisting, terrified at the very thought of having a conversation with such a pretty woman, an "older" woman at that. To put off the encounter, he persuaded his friend to go back to

Mead's, buy a snack, and then come back and talk to her, praying all the while that she would be gone when they returned.
When they came back a half-hour or so later at the most, as he
had hoped, she wasn't there. And as for the boy fishing at the
weir, he left during the time the other two boys were back at
Mead's, and he said that when he had packed up and left, night
had fallen, the moon had risen, and Alex was gone.

Here, the hollow blackness, the gap in the narrative appears.

Here, Alex went to meet her death, or more likely, by the
time the boy fishing at the weir had gone home, and the two
fifteen-year-olds had returned from the drugstore, she was
already dead. All of them went home, went quietly to their
beds and dreamt or did not dream of the pretty, small woman
at the weir, sitting on the concrete apron with her knees drawn
up and her arms embracing them, gazing out over the moon-
lit river. The entire small city, exhausted by spring's heady
onslaught, at last drifted off to sleep. Sometime after ten but
before midnight, a group of male university students who had
been drinking beer stopped their car on the north side of the
bridge and went below it to relieve themselves, but saw and
heard nothing, and were soon gone. No one living in any of
the houses across the road from the weir area heard so much as
a single unusual sound, certainly not a woman's screams.

Night fell, Alex was dead, the river flowed on, silver skimming its swift, flat darkness; its whispering murmur a heartbeat
away from language, it flowed on by, as it had for ten thousand
years, past her shallow grave in the sand, in a copse of trees on
the north side of the railway bridge.

❋

By midnight, her roommate Alice said, the hospital had called twice to ask where Alex was, a girl who was absolutely responsible about showing up for work, and precisely on time. Morning came without Alex's return, and Alice said, "I knew one hundred per cent that there was something really bad wrong," and another roommate, Pauline, the one who had been working until midnight, called the police. Someone, at some point, told her family, probably to see if they might know where she was, so the family was alerted to Alex's unheard-of failure to come home or to appear at work.

The family went out looking for her because the police would not, policy being that technically she was not yet a missing person, their belief being that she had probably gone off with a boyfriend and would show up within the next day or two. How terribly callous an attitude that seemed to her family and her friends, as it always seems to frightened, distraught families when a loved one fails to do as expected and/or goes missing. And all the while—although no one yet knew it—the clues that might have caught her killer were eroding, decaying, blowing away, beginning to dissolve in light rain.

When she did not come home, over the course of the next few days the police took two initiatives we know of. The first was on Wednesday, May 23, when they brought in a police dog to search the riverbank, that is, a dog belonging to a Saskatoon police officer that had been trained with the advice of an RCMP dog-handler but that was not an officially trained "police dog," and which found, a half-mile north of her grave, a discarded tissue the police believed had been Alex's, but nothing else. The second was ten days after she vanished, on Monday, May 28, when officers went by boat twenty-six miles downstream in search of her body or other evidence, and also found nothing.

It would be thirteen days before Alex was finally, officially, discovered by some children playing along the riverbank. They had found her a few days earlier, but when they told their father about the human hand they'd seen sticking out of the sand, he had paid no attention to them, occupied with his fishing, either not hearing what they said or disbelieving them. The second time the children told him, several days later, when they were again playing along the riverbank while he fished, he went with them to look, and seeing that they were right, he took the children home and, at last, called the police. It was just after 9 p.m. on May 31.

From that moment, the gap in the open, transparent life that had been Alex's began to narrow. Where she had been that day, what she had done, to whom she had said what, was slowly, bit by bit, over the next days and weeks, painstakingly reconstructed, and those who had seen her that night after she had left her home—at least, those of whom we know—reported, one by one, to the police and were questioned and sent away.

The details of what had happened to her can be cobbled together from newspaper reports, the autopsy report (done on June 1, 1962), and the transcript of the coroner's inquest (held on July 11 at the Saskatoon Police Station, the purpose of which was only to determine the cause of death). She was nude from the waist down with her slacks and underwear pushed down around her right ankle and that shoe still on her foot, but with the other lying nearby, and her blouse and brassiere had been torn apart down the centre. She had been raped, although the word was not used in the immediate newspaper accounts, as if either the police suspected she had had consensual intercourse and then been murdered, or more likely because, in keeping with the social codes of the time concerning a young lady, not a prostitute, this was a word too impolite to appear in print. Or perhaps because the pathologist had found only a tiny tear as damage to her sexual organs, although he found "numerous human male spermatozoa" in the upper part of the vagina. In any case, her knees were still flexed and her legs spread when she was found, which was surely the best indication of all.

She had sustained a punch in the face that had broken her nose and the sinuses behind it, pushed the nose into her face, and blackened her eye so that the right side of her face was unrecognizable with swelling and discolouration—"massive haemorrhage," the pathologist wrote. One of her teeth lay loose in her mouth. Her roommates, Alice and Doreen, had to identify her remains by the clothes she'd been wearing.

She had been hit on the head with an unidentified object—at least, unidentified to the public—it was not known how many times, perhaps only once, but so hard that her skull was fractured on the left side close to the centre, but nearer to the back of her skull—the parietal lobe—and all the skull's natural joins had fractured, then fallen back into position, leaving thin red lines where the joins had been. The autopsy report is not clear on the question of whether the brain was damaged at the front of the skull or only at the back, which fact would help determine the manner in which her skull was fractured. This was in part because, in the two weeks after her death, "autolysis" (the destruction of the cells by enzymes produced by the cells themselves), and putrefaction had occurred and her brain was "semi-fluid." The pathologist also told the coroner's inquest that these natural processes had "made the interpretation of many of the lesions very difficult." But earlier in his testimony, in response to a question, "And was there any specific damage to the brain, Doctor?" he replied, "All I could recognize was the blood on the surface of the brain and this was in close association with the fractures of the skull."

The pathologist, Dr. Ed Andres, who in only five years would be dead himself at forty-three of a brain tumour, leaving a wife and three young daughters, and who performed the autopsy, would tell the coroner's jury that to sustain that bad a skull fracture (or fractures), she would have had to fall ten or fifteen feet, so a blow or blows seemed more likely, but as there were many lacerations he could not tell if the instrument used had been, say, a hammer, and many blows with it, or something big and rough-edged (a concrete slab? a rock?) and one blow. In answer to a question, he said, yes, such a blow or blows would have knocked her unconscious.

The killer then buried her. The doctor knew he had done so while she was still alive because he had found dirt and sand in her mouth and windpipe—"oral cavity, pharynx, larynx, trachea and upper esophagus." She died, finally, he said, of asphyxiation, when she inhaled the sand and dirt of her grave. Dr. Andres' widow told me several times, when I met her in 2005, that she would never forget how upset her husband had been over this single fact—and it was the final, official conclusion of the inquest that Alex had died, not from the blows, but from asphyxiation.

The approximate time of death was determined by the contents of Alex's stomach, the light supper she had eaten with her roommate, Alice, and a neighbour, around 7 p.m. and which "showed very little change due to digestion." The length of time undigested food might remain in the stomach is normally about two hours, but can be as long as four.

The inquest concluded:

> Alexandria Wiwcharuk, residing at 1223–7th Avenue North, Saskatoon, Saskatchewan, died on May 18th, 1962 between the hours of 8:30 pm and 11:00 pm. Her body was found in a shallow grave about fifty feet north of the intersection of 33rd Street and Spadina Crescent on the river bank. The evidence shows she died as a result of asphyxia by the inhalation of earth and sand due to unconsciousness by blows to the head by some person or persons as yet unknown.

There is one more significant detail. She was found with a concrete slab resting on her chest below her chin. It was described as weighing "approximately thirteen pounds," and was ten inches by nine inches by three inches deep. The sergeant reporting on the investigation to the coroner's jury went on to say, "It was a broken piece of concrete with some yellow paint on one side which would indicate it came from a broken sidewalk," but he testified also that there was no blood found on it, indicating that it wasn't the object that had fractured her skull.

As nearly as I can tell, aside from the inquest stenographer, those presiding over events were all men: the six jurors, the coroner himself, and the agent representing the attorney general. The only time women appeared was when each of Alex's three roommates briefly testified. It is possible that one of Alex's brothers was present, but the family doesn't remember for sure, and the transcript doesn't say who might have attended the inquest; and if that brother did, he was the only family member there. And who exactly was representing Alex's interests and the family's interests? Presumably, that would be the agent for the attorney general, or the coroner himself. But, as "Jane Doe" concluded (she was the woman raped in Toronto twenty-four years later when the police did not warn about a rapist—she sued them and won), once the legal system goes into action, the victim can lose all importance.

Alex's funeral was held the afternoon of June 4. She was buried in Woodlawn Cemetery, where eventually both her parents would be interred, as would both my parents and one of my sisters, as would the doctor who had done her autopsy, the coroner, Dr. Whitemarsh, and a number of other people involved in the investigation. I considered going to her funeral but, in the end, decided I hadn't been close enough to her to justify asking for time off work.

I must have read the newspaper report of the inquest, but I have no memory of that at all, and I can hardly believe, in retrospect, that I didn't scream or cry or faint when I read that she had been buried alive. How "unconscious," as the Jungians say, I was in those days. Anything I didn't want to know, I simply didn't see. I had constructed a thick barrier between words and their meanings, and it would be quite a few years before I would teach myself that I had to tear that barrier down and allow myself to feel, no matter how painful, how horrible or sad—how very difficult it is to know the world as it really is. Feeling is a first leap toward wisdom. And it is the bane of an old person's existence to have to remember how unaware, how foolish, how cruel one was in one's youth.

In the weeks immediately after the discovery of Alex's body, the city waited breathlessly, stewing in rumour, suspicion, and fear, anxious for word from the police that they had caught Alex's killer. We all wanted then, and want now, to know the facts about her death; we have always wanted answers, wanted to dispel what feels like a mystery surrounding the simple fact of her murder. I tell the reader all these details, such as they are—I am sure they are incomplete—because only the broad outline of Alex's death has been revealed to the public in all these years, the coroner's report not having been released until the forty-fourth year after her murder. Rumours boil in the absence of facts; bad things happen because no one knows the truth. A police force loses the confidence of the citizens for whom it works, and then becomes insular, simmering in its own anger at the public's lack of confidence and disparagement of the force's abilities, despite the often tremendous efforts it makes. The police force grows surly, and the distance between it and the citizens widens, slowly, over years, becomes nearly unbridgeable.

When I came on the scene publicly in the late nineties, and in the next couple of years discovered that I could not expect help from the police beyond a brief recounting of a few of the bare facts, most of which I already knew, I turned to newspaper accounts, and to people who did know something. I was surprised by the stiff resistance I met from many of the police officers, old or new. The refusal of the police, even those who were retired, to assist me at all, struck me as merely proprietorial—the information was theirs and they would decide who would see it—rather than the result of any investigative necessity that the information continue to be kept secret (or, for that matter, because, as so many people told me they believed then, or would come to believe, that the police knew the identity of the killer or killers but had protected him or them). Alex's unsolved case has never been closed, and so refusal of information even after forty-four years makes some kind of legal sense, but I discovered that the Saskatoon police had also refused information to the lawyers of David Milgaard, who was already convicted of murder and had served many years in prison (for, it turned out, a crime he hadn't commit-ted). Even with the case closed they still refused information to his mother's lawyer. It's worth noting that the Canadian Charter of Rights and Freedoms didn't come into effect until April 17, 1982, and the Freedom of Information Act on July 1, 1983. Whether these would have made a difference, I don't know, but I hope that they would have.

If I was intimidated enough by 2003 to call in a national investigative television program, back in 1962 at least one member of the Wiwcharuk family was intimidated himself. A brother from Moose Jaw came to Saskatoon perhaps once a month with his wife and children, and would stay with his parents on their acreage south of Saskatoon. He told me that every time he was in town he would contact the police to ask how the investigation was going. On one occasion, as he was taking a shortcut east from the acreage to go onto the highway back to Moose Jaw, a car appeared to be waiting for him, and started to follow him. He likes to tell how he was driving a Mercury with a 390 horsepower motor—the biggest motor available in a car of that type then, and that had no shortage of power—so that as the car raced up to his back bumper with its headlights on high beam, making him extremely uneasy, rather than stopping he stepped on the gas. The track was narrow, and the car behind him speeded up too and seemed to be trying to get past him, and this Alex's brother was determined not to let happen. Then the car bumped his rear bumper. Frightened, he sped up even more—he says he was going nearly 110 miles per hour, with the car trying to catch him.

After some distance he changed his mind, deciding that the best move might be to let the car catch up so that he could see who was in it. He slowed, and the car pulled up parallel to him on his side. He says he saw the driver hand the passenger something, and the passenger began to roll down his window. He did not see the object, but believes to this day that it was a gun. He put his foot on the gas, expecting at any moment to hear shots, and with his car's superior power, easily left the other car behind. (Or perhaps the driver of the other car felt he had accomplished his purpose and let Alex's brother leave him behind.) Through his mirrors he could see the car behind him slow, make a U-turn, and go back to the city. He told me that he believes that no one but the family and the police knew he was in town.

Some years later, Alex's niece told me, she took a job working in the office of the doctor who had looked after Alex before her death. She told me that during her period of employment, perhaps a bit more than a year, one morning she arrived at work and unlocked the office door to find there had been a break-in during the night. All the doctor's many files were scattered everywhere, and when she looked, she told me, Alex's (which she said she had never looked inside, although she wanted to, perhaps even planned to) was gone. Nothing other than the files had been disturbed.

The family had become extremely suspicious of the police, and believing that it would do no good, never reported the car chase. Marie tells me that during the few months after Alex's death, when they asked for but received no information about the police investigation, the family discussed hiring a private detective, but that Mrs. Wiwcharuk said plaintively, "But the police are good, aren't they?" And so in the end, they decided against it, something they seem to have regretted ever since.

The people of Saskatoon still feel that the story of Alex's death is theirs—that is, that it belongs to the city as a whole, that it was a public event and is a part of our history. Professional historians didn't seem to think so, regarding it as too small, as inconsequential in the wide run of history, of the great sweep and movement of forces which have always been the subject of formal history. But in our provincial centennial year, 2005, Alex finally merited a line in a government-commissioned history book by Professor Bill Waiser of the University of Saskatchewan, *Saskatchewan: A New History*.

That her death made the pages of that book was in itself an historic event, and further, a sign of how the concept of what constitutes history is changing. Alex's murder had long been one of the events that defined the city of Saskatoon, and now Alex herself, that small, pretty Ukrainian girl, in a way no one ever would have predicted, had become—along with the explorers and the city founders, nearly all of them men—an historical figure. I cannot help but find it tragic and emblematic that a girl makes the history books not by her works, but by the combination of her beauty, and by getting herself raped and killed.

# Chapter Eight
## Evidence

As I pored over the original newspaper accounts, and the reprisals of the case in 1992, and then the documents of which I finally received copies, as well as viewing over and over again *Death of a Beauty Queen*, the documentary by CBC's *the fifth estate*, and talking to people about their recollections, I came across small discrepancies or inexplicable breaks in the chain of information.

For instance, Alex was found with that concrete slab on her chest, and everyone, myself included, seems to have taken it for granted that the slab was the murder weapon, although it was stated clearly that there was no blood on it. (Even the term *murder weapon* is inaccurate, because the inquest jury concluded absolutely that Alex died of asphyxiation, not directly by the blows to the head.) Perhaps even the police, to this day, do not know what instrument broke her skull. Or perhaps they do. But if the slab wasn't the weapon, one has to wonder what it was doing on her chest.

Then there was the dog search on Wednesday, May 23, a week before her body was officially found ("a tracking dog . . . came within 600 feet of the grave. Police . . . worked the dog south along the west side of the river. . . ," it said in the *Star Phoenix*, June 2, 1962). The exact route of the dog search isn't given, and its fruitlessness was explained at the inquest by the fact that there had been a lot of rain just before it. But I searched out the official weather records from Environment Canada for that two weeks in May 1962, between when Alex disappeared and when her body was found, and they state that there had been only "1.6 millimetres" between May 18 and 23, and that the heavier rains didn't occur until a week after, on the 29 and 30. (Not to mention that testimony at the inquest by a police officer made clear that this was not a formally trained police dog.) Although the officer assured the coroner that the dog could be trusted, people who should know doubt it.

The riverbank area where she was murdered and buried by her killer was in the process of being scraped by large machinery for some purpose. A full landscaping couldn't have been the plan because even today it is still a wild-looking area. But newspaper photos of the time show that a wide swath of sloping riverbank between the edge of Spadina Crescent and the second, steeper drop to the river below had been completely denuded except for that one small, compact island of trees about fifty feet from the north side of the bridge in which Alex's body was found. A small cabin-like structure on wheels on the copse's western edge, belonging to the city's construction crew, had been there, the inquest was told, for two weeks or so as the men worked on the riverbank.

The deep scraping by a bulldozer, testified to by one of the investigating officers, which he offered as reason both for the failure of the dog's search and for the lack of evidence at the site—saying that all tracks were destroyed—is contradicted by a wide-angle newspaper photo taken after Alex's body was found. It clearly shows tire tracks on both sides of the copse, although from such a distance one can only guess whether those tracks might be those of a bulldozer, or of police cars, or of the ambulance that, presumably, would have gone down there to pick up poor Alex's remains. I would eventually read in documents not released to the public that tire tracks were indeed found that night by the copse where her body was discovered. As well, I have some vague memory of a date of mine driving me down there late one night—although I've forgotten when that happened—showing that lots of people must have done that, and that such tracks weren't necessarily connected to the killing.

Also in the RCMP lab report, done between the finding of Alex's body and the inquest, is an analysis of "sweepings" from the front and back seat of "a 1950 Dodge," and in the absence of any other material about these "sweepings," I am guessing they could be related to the tire tracks near the copse. Or maybe they were from her boyfriend's car, or the car of some other person who was seen as a suspect but never identified as such to the public.

That the police felt keenly their failure to catch the killer seems clear to me from a 1992 newspaper interview with a retired officer, since deceased, who had been an integral part of the 1962 investigation. The officer declared—as if to reassure us once again how hard the force had tried—that at the beginning, all of the 130 police officers were working double duty. But the detective sergeant at the 1962 inquest testified that during June, ten men had been on the case, and in July, four of them—that is, that many men on each shift worked around the clock. If the retired officer's hyperbole shows anything, I think, it is only how the force's inability to solve this one case would not go away, how even in 1992 it still worried and upset them, and how deep was their desire, still, to find Alex's killer. Decent men, fathers, thinking perhaps of their own daughters, as well as how they had failed in their duty to the public, to Alex, and to her family.

Most striking of all, some forty-two years later, the police would indicate in the television documentary that among the gathered evidence there was "a bunch of dark reddish brown hair, thirty strands, approximately four to five inches in length." (Specifically, what the officer said was, "They've got down here . . ."—"here" being on the list of evidence dated May 31, 1962, from which he was reading.) The viewers don't see the hair, although it might have been in the brown business-size envelope with handwriting on it which can't be read by the viewer, but family and friends know that Alex's hair was black. I froze at this news, and the media certainly was excited by it, because with the new DNA technology, surely a profile of her killer could be obtained. But I was puzzled that there was no mention of this particular swatch of hair on any of the documents I saw from 1962.

And there seems to have been hair everywhere. The autopsy stated that much of it was missing from Alex's scalp, but what remained was black. There were fifty-five "scalp hairs . . . ranging in colour from medium light brown to dark brown on her sweater," and another "forty-four hairs scalp hairs [sic] . . . ranging in colour from light brown to dark brown" on her blouse, "seven medium brown scalp hairs" on her bra, "three scalp hairs and one pubic hair" on or in her slacks, "a tuft of approximately 100 scalp hairs ranging in colour from light brown to dark brown and ranging in length from 2″ to 7″. . . inside the [right] shoe." The lab also reported that "ten medium to dark brown scalp hairs and two dark brown pubic hairs were removed from the narrow edge on the piece of concrete," the one that had been resting on her chest.

Sergeant Sam Holoboff, Identification Section, Saskatoon Police Service, when testifying at the coroner's inquest, in response to being asked to read the "salient points" from the RCMP lab report, listed all these hair samples, but did not mention the approximately one hundred hairs found in her right shoe, from two to seven inches long and described as light brown to dark brown (not "dark reddish brown"). I was baffled, because surely these hairs were the most significant piece of evidence. Finally, I asked a criminal lawyer about the rules of evidence regarding the coroner's inquest and was told that "there is nothing to say that the police have to give *all* the evidence to the coroner." On the other hand, it is undeniable that what seems to be a discrepancy might only have been a matter of semantics. (What is "light" brown, or "reddish" brown, or "dark" brown? Maybe the labs then had a standard descriptive scale to which they matched items of evidence.)

Although the media said she had been "clutching" these hairs—contradicting the RCMP lab report which makes no mention at all of Alex being found holding hair, nor does the autopsy report mention such a thing, nor did the transcript from the inquest—the police, when they mentioned the hair publicly, never said specifically (that I am able to locate) that she had been "clutching" the thirty strands of dark reddish brown hair.

If the purpose of the coroner's inquest is only to determine the cause of death, then such an omission seems less puzzling. And yet, why would it matter whether the public knew the police had a goodly sample of the probable-killer's hair? I suppose because if the killer was still there in the city and read, in the newspaper report of the inquest proceedings, that the police could identify him by his hair, he would be gone from the city as fast as was humanly possible.

But in 1962 the only way to identify hair was by visual examination under the microscope for a comparison of "morphological" features. One of the girls who attended Tech with Alex and me, and who during high school had been my close friend, had become a laboratory technician and eventually the manager of a prestigious lab. I called to ask her for advice. She said, "Forget 1962." No conclusions arrived at by way of hair identification in the 1962 RCMP lab report, used at the inquest, would necessarily hold today. "Now it's all about DNA," she told me.

But in the end the lab had concluded, carefully,

> All scalp and pubic hairs removed from the clothing
> . . . as well as the scalp and pubic hairs removed from
> the concrete block . . . are similar in morphologi-
> cal features to the scalp and pubic hairs [taken from
> Alex's remains, that were definitely hers] . . . and could
> have originated from the same respective source, or
> any other source subscribing to similar morphologi-
> cal features.

Which means, what? That they could have been Alex's as they looked rather like hers, but that they could have been somebody else's too.

Aside from the hair swatch, the host of *Death of a Beauty Queen*, Linden McIntyre, tells the viewer that the nail scrapings from Alex's hands contained "skin she ripped from the body of her attacker." The 1962 RCMP lab report doesn't mention skin, but it does record that the left-hand nail scrapings are "soil like material and 24 hairs," the longest of which is 1 1/4" in length, a scalp hair, and dark brown; the remainder were less than 1/4" in length and light brown; and the nail scrapings from the right hand are "soil like material and three hairs," one of which is pubic hair and is 2 1/4 inches long, but no colour is given. I'm guessing that the "soil like material" is the skin mentioned in the documentary, but the lab report, after describing the scrapings, doesn't mention them again, other than to indicate that they'd been sent to the serology lab, which reported only that there was no blood on the hair. The "soil like material" vanishes from that record.

My only safe conclusion from all of the above material is that the police, even then, were carefully managing what information got out to the public, and it appears to me that the agent for the attorney general had some of this information and was co-operating in not revealing that the police had it. I am also told, reliably, that in Saskatchewan in 1962 the relationship between the attorney general's agent and the police force in the person of the chief was a hazy one, which has since been more clearly defined. There was then, apparently, a lot of room for discretion as to what would be revealed and what would not to the coroner's inquest, and to how closely the attorney general's agent and the police chief worked in making such decisions.

I wondered why no witnesses to Alex's movements that night, other than the three roommates, were called to testify at the inquest. By July 11, the day of the inquest, the young husband who had driven past Alex and the tall, "well-built" man had identified himself to the police and told his story, as had the two young boys who stood above and behind Alex at the weir, admiring her but afraid to talk to her. The police apparently soon located the boy who had been fishing at the weir and spoke to him as well. But none of them were called to testify. I thought that, in view of the pieces of evidence I was finding that weren't revealed to the inquest, perhaps this was because those who decided who would be called wouldn't call witnesses that would reveal information that—

it had been decided—needed to be kept secret in order to catch the killer.

But it turns out that the decision as to who would be called as witnesses was made by the office of the attorney general. I asked this question of someone whose life is the law, and after answering me, he went on to remark, as a "by the way" that he thought I might find interesting, that at one time a common abuse at coroner's inquests (in cases where homicide was the cause of death) had been the practice of having the strong suspects appear as witnesses. "The Supreme Court put a stop to that," he told me, amused by the ploy. And I couldn't help but think how, if you spent your life in courtrooms and reading law and talking about cases, you would soon learn detachment, you would soon learn to be wearily amused. At the time, I didn't even make a note of this remark, but did so later, having been wondering since I first read of the inquest in an old newspaper clipping why the boys who had seen Alex at the riverside after she'd mailed her letters hadn't been called as witnesses. Now I thought I knew: one or all of them were seen as suspects.

Besides the hair and the dog search and the witnesses and so on, the inquest heard that Alex had had at least one phone call at around 10 p.m., long after she had left the apartment. Alice had taken the call:

> Q: Was this a boy friend—or a man friend?
> A: Yes.
> Q: And you couldn't tell us who it was—but did you know him?

A: Yes.

Q: And what was he phoning about?

A: He was trying to make a double date for the next evening to go somewhere.

The statement "And you couldn't tell us who it was—" is puzzling, as it is apparent the witness *did* know who the caller was. It must have been decided ahead of time that she was not to say the caller's name aloud. As no one asked what the man's name was, I can only guess that everyone else present had agreed not to reveal it.

There is more to the story, but some of it seems trivial or irrelevant, and some of it is hard to find a place for in this narrative. For instance, in January 2004 when *the fifth estate* aired its documentary, one of those interviewed was a man who had been dating Alex at the time of her disappearance (and who, in 1964, became a Saskatoon police officer, from which work he is now retired). He tells the interviewer that he called Alex that fateful night to find out if he could drive her to work (from my memory of being young in Saskatoon then, this was probably a euphemism for what today would be called "a make-out session," especially since it was only a twelve- or thirteen-minute walk from Alex's apartment to work), but that she "had gone out to mail a letter," indicating that someone had answered the phone—and suggesting now that there were possibly two phone calls from men, not just the one mentioned at the inquest.

And as this man billed as Alex's boyfriend—who may have

been only one of several dating her—had left the city the next morning to spend the weekend with friends (unless Alex had to work the next night too, and so he had decided to go to Waskesiu), he wasn't the one who phoned about double dating the next night. He says, in the taped 2004 interview, that he "hadn't been in Waskesiu very long before the RCMP came by to talk to me, to see if Alex was with me and whether I knew anything more about where she might be." But the Wiwcharuk family didn't think the police were looking for Alex yet, as she had been gone only overnight, and the reporter for the *Star Phoenix* says on the same tape that "the police weren't bothering with that file at all." Although considerable allowance has to be made for the vagaries of memory after forty-some years, it seems to me that police were already playing their cards very close to their chests, maybe too close, because they were doing a lot of work behind the scenes and telling no one about it—work which, to this day, remains a carefully kept secret.

The investigation took an unusual turn when sixteen-year-old Billy McGaffin, who'd been fishing alone on the apron of the dam the night of the murder (or I would think he was alone until late in 2006 when I would find out differently), in an effort to ferret out more precise memories, was hypnotized at the request of the police by Saskatoon doctor Lewis Brand. Retired officer Hugh Fraser, according to the

1992 newspaper account, says that he was skeptical about such a technique, but when the boy gave a thorough description of Alex, especially of the shoes Alex had been wearing when he saw her at around 9:30 p.m., he lost his skepticism. That particular detail—the colour and type of shoe—he said, had been withheld from the media.

The boy also said that Alex had left the riverbank shortly after 10 p.m., and that there had been "another person, alone, sitting on the apron at the north end." This newspaper account says that the tape of the hypnosis session by then had disappeared from the file, but that at the time of the writing, fourteen years ago, the transcript of the tape was still on file. There was no tape when the CBC's *the fifth estate* did their documentary in 2004, and they used actors reading from the transcript.

Under hypnosis, the youth described two cars he had seen parked along Spadina Crescent at the apron, at roughly the same time. One of these was an older model, two-tone "Ford-type" car with three teenage boys in it. The documentary goes on to say that "another witness reported seeing a similar car later that night parked across from where the body was found two weeks later." The second car the hypnotic subject saw was a red sports car with one man in it. The two boys—or rather, the one of them, as I made no attempt to contact the friend who had been with him that night—who had been too shy to talk to Alex say they did not see either car, either time they were at the weir.

According to the CBC's documentary, Dr. Brand asked the boy who was hypnotized whether he saw anyone else there, and he responded that there was the older car with the three boys in it. According to the transcript, Dr. Brand asked no more questions about the older car, but instead inquired whether the boy had seen any other vehicles there. The boy responded about the red sports car, and Dr. Brand, oddly, did not return to the first car. But the RCMP lab report states clearly that the contents of the front seat and the back seat of a 1950 Dodge were examined for evidence, not those of a red sports car. Whether the 1950 Dodge was or was not the older, two-tone "Ford-type" car, or some other car entirely, I don't know. Once again, of course, we might be dealing with an incomplete transcript, a precaution possibly taken so that the information the police were most concerned with as signifi- cant did not fall into the hands of the public.

In February 2006, I was allowed to read Hugh Fraser's "Investigation Report" dated June 1, 1962. It was written at 4:40 a.m., and in it he says that after midnight he, along with Dr. Slobodian (Alex's doctor) and Father Bodnarchuk, went to notify Alex's parents. He also records that Alex's brother- in-law told the police that a man who worked at the hospital and who drove a red convertible had kept trying to take Alex out, and that when she refused, he would follow her. As well, her brother-in-law named a man with a red car who tried to go out with her, but Fraser writes that it is not known if these were the same man. Thus, the "red car" lead was clearly among the very first.

The police then pursued the driver of the red car, and with little effort found it. (The CBC tells me that there were only two cars of that type in Saskatoon at that time.) Today, my old girlfriends say to me in astonishment with regard to the driver of that car, "Don't you remember him? He was always giving us rides, but nobody would go out with him. We told him that. He knew we'd never be anything more than friends." Since discussing this with these friends I dredged up a very old memory of perhaps in grade twelve being offered a ride by him, and, having heard about him from my girlfriends, turning him down. He didn't persist, not even seeming surprised at my refusal. I also have a vague memory of hesitating for a split second as I gazed at his gorgeous little car. But relatives of mine knew him, and while everyone else who knew him insists he was harmless, my relatives were wary of him—although they also say that he never did anything they knew of to validate their wariness.

The man who owned the red car was Ukrainian, but he went by an Anglicized version of his name. His misfortune was to have picked a surname that happened also to be that of a prominent Saskatoon-area family whose members included a lawyer and a judge. Today, people think that because of that surname he was confused by the public with the prominent family. In the absence of a killer being found, a few people decided he was the guilty man and that the police hadn't named him because the high status of his family protected him. It seems to me that if the police didn't suspect him, they would have done well to let the public know. On the other hand, maybe they deliberately fostered that rumour or simply failed to correct it, to divert the public's interest in the true investigation, which was, by then, going in a different direction.

The "son or sons of a prominent man or men" theory surfaced again and again in my question-asking. A CBC researcher was supposedly told by somebody that Dr. Brand (who hypnotized Billy McGaffin for the police) said to some-one in a bar one night after the hypnosis session that this one would never be solved because the rape, beating, and killing had been done by not one son of one prominent man, but by—as far as I can remember—three sons of three prominent men. Dr. Brand, who had been forced to retire under a cloud some years later, died in 1994 and there is no proof he ever said this.

In the end, I concluded that there were two rumours: the "son of a prominent man" who drove the red car, and the "sons of prominent men" who, I guess, were driving a differ-ent car, quite likely the older-model "Ford-type" car. Beyond this, the rumours twisted and turned and mixed in with each other, and some parts were believed by some people, and other parts by other people, the only consistency being the "son(s) of prominent man/men").

Looking back over all the many stories I'd heard, the theo-ries, the rumours, and especially the twin beliefs that dogged Saskatoon—that the police didn't know what they were doing and thus failed, and its opposite, that the police knew who had killed Alex but had their own, of course, devious reasons for not identifying him—I began to see that almost certainly nei-ther was true. The police had investigated, as they had always said, thoroughly, and were continuing to do so, and although they had strong suspicions and evidence that seemed to back them, they did not know with certainty, any more than the public did, who had killed Alex.

One day in 2006 I realized that it had been twenty years since I had had that strange dream about my diary resting on the pedestal in the Ukrainian Hall which had, in the dream, become a museum; it had been ten years since I first began asking questions, since the first time I'd looked up the old reports in the *Star Phoenix*. I had files everywhere in my office, three or four notebooks, and a scattering of bits of paper with scribblings on them that mostly no longer made much sense to me. All the stories I'd heard, the rumours people told me, the newspaper reports, the documents I'd finally received, were running through my head—too many details to capture and hold steady, too many versions to isolate and separate, many of which I couldn't reconcile from report to report, and the discrepancies which I couldn't explain. I pitied the police who had ten times the material to deal with, and a "file" containing something like eleven hundred names.

In fact, I fell into a trap: I had allowed myself to be so seduced by the mystery of Alex's death that my original intention, to answer some not-quite-defined question about what had happened that night, led me off into this minute examination of documents, into questioning people, into studying the CBC tape as if I were a private investigator hired to solve the murder—and every question I asked calling up a dozen more that I felt I had to try to answer to get the "complete" picture. And, of course, the truth was that sitting in my office five hours from Saskatoon, without access to all the available information, without the right to know who the suspects were, or what the evidence was, I could never "solve" the murder.

Still, I pondered what had been done to Alex. I tried to reconstruct the beating, rape, and murder, as police officer after police officer must have done: Which came first, the punch in the face that had destroyed her beauty, or the blow or blows to her skull? Was she conscious when she was raped? Or unconscious? Or had there been consensual intercourse first? I asked myself these questions over and over again, along with all the variations on the sequence of events that the reader can well imagine. I wondered: Was there only one attacker? Or two, or more? Did she get into a car or was she dragged into one? Or was no car involved at all? Did she know her attacker (or them), or was he (or them) a stranger? *Fascinated, obsessed*— these words, I finally admitted, did indeed apply to me.

One day, as for the umpteenth time over what was now years I went over my pieces of paper, I began to feel fatigue take hold of me. My mind had stopped functioning, refused to respond to my efforts to be rational, logical. I closed my eyes, pressed my fingers against them, and rested my elbows on each side of my laptop, feeling the ache in my back of which I'd just become aware. Such weariness, an immense fatigue, of a kind I had never before experienced. It was beyond the merely physical, beyond even a mental fatigue, reaching deep inside me, I think now, down into my soul.

The moment had come when the pettiness of the details, the viciousness, the ugliness of them began to seem not fascinating, not vital, not even interesting or disgusting, but in some odd, futile way—*boring*. They had become banal. And it was then that I saw what Hannah Arendt meant when, the year after Alex's death, she pronounced this odd word about the Nazi horrors. Now I saw her meaning, and I saw that she was right; it might not be the whole truth, but it was correct as far as it went. By this, I mean that I grew weary of the details, their quality of eternal repetitiveness, that the killing of one human being by another, or the torture of one by another, is all too wearily commonplace, and the details all too similar.

The illogicality, the cruelty of that word *banal* to describe the evil of Alex's death was absolutely clear to me, just as the aptness, the accuracy of it was now, too. But because I knew all too well that every detail of exactly how Alex died was not banal, mattered a great deal to the one who had suffered them, as it did to those who had truly loved her, I found that I could not reconcile these opposites—the one accepting the ineradicable presence of evil on earth, and the other demanding with perfect righteousness, *Know exactly how I died; honour my death.*

## Chapter Nine
## Sorrow

Alex was, in certain ways, not just a beloved daughter. She was also the first to get an education, to acquire a profession, both of which she did very well, and then to lift herself from the common herd with the combination of her vibrant personality, her joy in life, and her beauty. She had been a kind of beacon for the family, a special point of pride, and also, an answer to the then too-prevalent prejudice against Slavs, and as such, a triumph for her community.

But I imagine that for her parents and brothers and sisters, Alex was just that dear little girl they had lost. I come from a family of five children, and if my youngest sister, who as a baby, a toddler, a child was the most beloved of all of us, had met the death Alex met at barely twenty-three, I know it would have altered our family forever, and scarred each of us individually. It is not a place I like to go, even if only in my imagination. But I think that from the moment of the news of her death, everything any of us ever did, or thought, or dreamt of, would be coloured by the knowledge of our beloved's hideous end, that we would see in our minds, all of us, unwillingly, helplessly, over and over again, that scene we hadn't been present for (and all the more endlessly terrible because we did not see it)—the blows, the blood, the screams—until we had to pull our imaginations away, to save ourselves. That we would be, every one of us, in some way wounded, although with a wound no one else could see, and that our view of the world in which we all find ourselves would be irreparably and forever altered.

Evil would enter our world view, if it was not already there. And the bitter understanding that evil is implacable and without pity, without compassion. That there is no answer to it, no adequate response to it. There is belief in goodness, there is prayer, but no matter how high the mountain of goodness, or of prayer, evil remains.

And so some family members I spoke to were still angry; they were deeply, profoundly angry, at her death, at the police for not catching the killer; perhaps they were angry at the world in a more general way. Others, I think, must have been permanently saddened. That is, I had a sense of that shock and unhappiness having transmuted itself from that immediate raging grief—of a sort we all know, and know cannot be lived with, that must change—into a deep, diffuse sorrow that remained and would remain until death.

Others could not let the investigation go, could not let go of the need to find the killer. Yet, I saw this as just another way of begging the world, or the universe, or God, or the good angels, either to return Alex to them, or, failing that, to explain why she had had to die so brutally, when she was so young, and without any of them with her to hold her and pray for and with her as she died. So that she might have gone surrounded by love, and not by evil.

All of this happened forty-four years ago as I write this, and most of Alex's immediate family have grown old; both Alexander Wiwcharuk, Alex's father, and her mother, Anna, have died. Those who were children and living in Saskatoon then were probably not a part of the family events the night that Alex's body was found, or would have been too young to have clear memory of them. So when I asked for certain details, carefully, gently, and found what I thought were contradictions in sequence or in details, I did not pursue them. How could they possibly matter now? Add to this the fact that the family was in the middle of a terrible trauma and trying to assimilate it during the time I was asking questions about, and it is no wonder that I am not sure of the sequence of events for them that night.

Marie says that she heard about the finding of her sister's body on the radio at about ten o'clock in the evening—the police received the phone call about the discovery at 9:05 p.m.—and she immediately called the police to have it confirmed. I asked her—this was over the phone some weeks after our meeting—who had told her parents. She thought for a moment. "I guess I did," she said in her forceful way, with what sounded like surprise in her tone, as if, not having thought about this for a very long time, she had just remembered. She and her husband, Robert, must have gone to her parents' home a few miles south of Saskatoon to tell them. (Although, she also told me that she was so distraught that a nurse who was a friend came and sat with her for hours, until she was calmer. Yet, distraught or not, I can't imagine Marie, the eldest daughter, not insisting on being with her parents, her mother in particular, at the moment of their receiving this news.)

Alex's mother, when she was told, screamed and then fainted. By this time, according to Marie, Anna Wiwcharuk had had intimations that her daughter had died. As she lay sleepless in bed one night during that interminable thirteen-day wait for news, she told her family that she had felt something heavy fall across her feet.

The sister closest to Alex in age, Ann, wrote to me that in the days following the news, Alex's mother would read the newspaper account aloud of how "Alexandra's head was bashed in and [she was] buried alive." She would cry as she read it, until Ann would beg her, "Mama, don't read any more today." Every day family members would take her to her daughter's grave at the cemetery where she would cry inconsolably until the family would have to take her home. Night after night, Ann reports, Anna could not sleep for crying, until finally, one night as she lay awake in her bed, Alexandra appeared at its foot. Smiling down at her mother, she said, tenderly, "Mama, don't cry any more. I'm okay now, Mama, don't cry any more." It was only after that that her mother was able to stop her steady weeping. A strong woman, she did not die until thirty years after her daughter, and a few years after the death of her husband. Perhaps she was waiting for the capture of Alex's killer; perhaps she was waiting for justice.

I wonder, too, if she did not sometimes think of her beloved Alex's life being bracketed by two startling and wonderful visions: Alex as a newborn, yet an angel hovering above her mother's bed, and Alex in her death, coming from the other side—from heaven, I'm sure Anna thought—to comfort her heartbroken mother.

Pearl, on hearing the news, is said to have wept inconsolably "for a month," and in her grief, unable to eat, lost fifteen pounds. Alex's brothers, understandably, felt that if they could only find the killer they would like to wreak justice on him themselves. Ann, by this time, had small children and lived in Ontario. She was too upset to attend the funeral by herself, and had to wait until her husband could get time off work so that he could go with her to her parents' home in Saskatoon. She wrote to me, "I cannot put into words the pain and suffering, the hours of crying, the missing of her and thinking and hurting, thinking how she must have suffered. It was as if the world should have stopped turning and life should have stopped. How could people get up and go to work when this terrible tragedy had happened?"

As the days after Alex's death passed, the funeral came and went without bringing much relief, and as the police questioned them, and they the police, trying to get any news at all about the progress of the investigation, the family had much opportunity to go over their last visits with Alex, their memories of their final conversations, their sense of how Alex had been feeling and thinking about her life. I imagine them gathering at their parents' home, sitting around the kitchen table, or perhaps in the living room, seated on the sofa or straight-backed kitchen chairs, quietly, staring into space, then someone interrupting the heavy silence to speak softly, *She said to me* . . . or *I just remembered that* . . . or, *But if she said she was going to, then why* . . . And other family members chiming in to agree or disagree, or to elaborate.

Marie would have told them that this long weekend in May Alex really wanted to go to Marie's camp at Emma Lake, and was disappointed because she had to work. Ann would have told them that she had had what she felt was an odd communication from Alex. In a letter to Ann—this was probably one of the letters Alex had mailed the night of her disappearance—Alex wrote that she felt uneasy, restless, and was thinking about moving somewhere else. Then she had ended the letter, saying that she would write more next time. Ann would have told them, as she wrote to me all these many years later, that she felt that something was telling Alex to leave the city, that Alex had had a premonition that she was in danger.

Did they have theories of their own? Did they weave scenarios? Did it always come back to that moment when Alex lay bleeding, battered, dying in the dirt of the riverbank? And then, one of the sisters, beginning to sob quietly, and Alexander Wiwcharuk rising abruptly, pushing back his chair noisily, walking fast across the floor to the door, maybe Anna calling his name, going outside, letting the door bang shut, striding across the yard, disappearing around a corner or an outbuilding where he would give full vent to his helpless rage, his grief. And inside, again, the thick, baffled, and pain-filled silence falling.

Alexandra's mother would tell the family that the last time she saw Alex, Alex had come to visit them. She had been dressed up because her boyfriend would come later to pick her up for a date. He arrived as planned, and Alexander and Anna walked with them out to the car. I imagine the family listening intently as Anna went on, speaking in Ukrainian, gesturing—or perhaps not—her hands folded and still on her lap as she talked. As Alex's boyfriend opened the car door for her, her mother asked her, "When will I see you again?" Alex smiled, then, with a laugh—I can see her, pretty as a picture, secure in her knowledge of her mother's love for her, toss-ing her head, her dark eyes sparkling—replied teasingly, "Well, maybe never." But Anna Wiwcharuk would tell the family that she felt a cold shiver go through her at this. As she looked at the man standing there, holding open the car door for Alex, she thought suddenly that dressed all in dark clothing as he was, he looked like an attendant who stands by a hearse.

But Anna Wiwcharuk would also tell her family that Alex had told her that she had caught a nurse stealing drugs, that Alex had reported this to the hospital authorities, and that the nurse had threatened her for doing so, saying something to the effect that Alex would pay for having reported her. Then she, or perhaps a brother or a sister, would tell them all how at Orthodox Easter, Alex had gone to church with her parents, and after the service, as they stood on the church steps, Alex gazed around and said, suddenly, "I feel that some-one is following me." They would all recall, shaking their heads, numb with the certainty of their failure, that later that day they had taken her back to her apartment, and none of them had looked any further into her remark.

And, the family discovered, Alex had left a diary. It was written in a code, Marie explained to me, and she had tried and tried to read it, but couldn't. When the police heard of its existence, a young police officer Marie described to me only as "a family friend" came over and "begged" to be allowed to see it. Marie said she didn't want to give it to him, but eventu-ally she did. A week or so later, he returned it to her, telling her that it had taken the force a week to break the code. Sit-ting in my office in the Frenchman Valley, in the rural silence, as we talked on the phone, I longed to ask Marie, "What did the diary say?" but I could not bring myself to do it. I sup-pose now that I thought Marie—if she knew—would at some point tell me about its contents, that I shouldn't pressure her to tell me. But she went on to say that its very existence distressed her so much, as did the fact that against her better judgement she had let the police read it, that she burned it.

Later, she would mention in passing that in the diary, Alex hadn't named anyone. "There were no names," she said, her voice heavy. "Just . . . 'the handsome one', or 'the tall one,' and so on." Such emotion was in her voice, although I couldn't quite decipher it. "They tell me I shouldn't have burned it," she went on, I thought with a touch of anger, or perhaps a certain rueful-ness. It seemed to me that more than anything it was because, in her deep love for her sister, it so offended her that anyone not of the family would read, indeed would pore over words—no matter how meaningless, how innocent—her sister had meant for no one else's eyes. It might have seemed just another way that Alex would be stolen from them, the closeness of their family, their shared lives and memories, and once again violated.

Alex had just turned twenty-three; by the time I was twenty-one I was married, by my twenty-third year I was pregnant, as was true of many of the girls with whom we'd both gone to high school, some of whom by then had two or three children. With jobs—those of us who had jobs, as I did—and husbands, and children to care for, we had no time for diaries, much less time to devise and write one in code, even if such had been our inclination. I am sure that for all of us, diaries were a thing of our early teens, and I wonder why a woman of her age would still be keeping a diary: Was it because she had a secret, or secrets? Because she had no one she felt she could trust with her secrets? And were her secrets only her dreams of a better, more glamorous, more exciting life? Or were they about her private, intimate life—sexual history, for example—and she did not want anyone to know the details?

How well I remember, at nineteen, at two o'clock in the morning after a date, sitting in my good dress on the top step of the stairs, on either side of which were the bedrooms where my sisters were sleeping, hugging my knees, trying to accept that the first man I'd ever loved had told me that he was leaving and would not be taking me with him; not able to cry, nor to sleep, absorbed in the dull pain filling my chest, and wondering how I would ever be happy again. Feeling, too, shame, wondering how I would tell my sisters and my parents that I'd been abandoned by the man they knew I loved. If I'd had a journal I might have written in it about what had happened, and how I felt, but I had no journal then. I doubt that Alex ever sat alone in the middle of the night, trying to absorb the fact that the man she loved had left her forever. What man would leave an Alex? And if that kind of love had touched Alex, why was she not married? But, whatever was in the diary, apparently the police did not see a need to keep the original.

My first thought on hearing that Marie had burned it was one of profound regret. My regret is more that we lost a document that might have told us—me, and our mutual friends— much more about what was going on in Alex's mind and heart, and for that, there could never be a replacement. It is hard not to think of Anne Frank's priceless, touching diary that gave the world a record of the person she was, that made her appalling death all the more heartbreaking and tragic; for countless future generations, she could stand in for all the other many girls we know nothing about but who died in the same brutal way. Who knows but Alex's diary might one day have done the same for young women of another time and place, another life.

Sometime after the reading of the diary, Marie tells me that a police officer meeting with some of the family made a remark to the effect that perhaps they had not known Alex as well as they thought they did. I was taken aback, as I'm sure the family had been, although Marie did not elaborate. I wondered what he could have meant by that cryptic statement.

Suddenly I understood. Of course the police—they were all men after all—had to have worked from the point of view that Alex was not an innocent, virginal girl, but that she had, or might have, slept with a number of men. It would have been (as it was for the public) the first thing they considered: Had she brought on her own death by being too available to men, by being "easy"? And its corollary, a product of the time, yes, but a point of view that still exists (for example, among many examples, the failure of the Vancouver Police to pay much attention to the missing women, many of whom worked in the sex trade, who were murdered on the pig farm outside Vancouver), that a sexually active, unmarried woman is a woman who has lost her value, who need not be respected. That her family need not be respected because they were blind to the "probability" that Alex was not "pure."

I had wondered myself about her virginity, and I thought I had detected a clear but also failed attempt by the doctor who had performed the autopsy to determine if she'd been a virgin, one of the serious questions the police would have wanted answered. Having failed to determine this, they would have begun hunting out the men who knew her, and interviewing them to find out, among other things, whether she had slept with them or not.

The question was, as the writer of her story, and supposing (but not knowing) it to be true, in what way would it change my attitude? I thought hard for a moment: Not at all. As it should not have changed the point of view of the police. It was irrelevant, except in the pinpointing of men who would have had the motive and the opportunity to be her killer. Further, even if it were true, she did not "deserve" to be murdered.

So the Wiwcharuk family, in the atmosphere of heightened tension of that summer in Saskatchewan (the medicare crisis was underway, and the doctors' three-week strike), in its unrelenting dry heat, and while the investigation went on in secrecy around them, continued questioning the police, and at home in their shared sorrow, their long, pained discussions, their sometimes weeping, and sometimes rage, their bafflement and desperation, struggled to come to terms with Alex's death, and its inexplicable viciousness. Every day, each of them woke, wondering, *Is today the day the police will catch her killer?* Or perhaps, before they were even fully awake, thinking of her, they half-expected to open their eyes and find her standing in the room with them, or to hear her cheerful laugh just outside the bedroom door. And when they did not, when the reality of her death slowly sank into them one more time, I am sure that they started each day in a heavy sadness.

All of this might have been mitigated had the extensive police investigation not been, in the end, fruitless. To be able to see the killer, to know his name, to hear his whining, lying reasons—or lack of them—for doing what he had done. To be able to spit on him and curse him and revile him until all such need to do so had worn away, or the final futility of such actions had been made irrefutably clear. Then to see him put in prison forever would have helped them all immeasurably to come to terms with Alex's loss. It would not have brought her back, and no explanation from the killer would ever suffice, and no punishment ever be enough, but his capture, his public naming, the shared revulsion of the public, would have helped them find, as people like to say, peace. Or if not peace, perhaps (as I am more inclined to think) resignation, perhaps even acceptance of the inscrutability of fate.

In August 2004 the police exhumed Alex's remains. I know this because I had developed the habit of stopping by her grave whenever I was in town. This time, I had taken a bouquet of roses, a deep red that reminded me of her beauty queen bouquets, and the one she carried in the picture of her graduation from nursing, although not as dark a shade. This colour because somehow it reminded me of her, and of her youth and her beauty at her death. This time I brought flowers because I wanted her to know that I would be honourable, that I understood that the only right I had to her story would come from being faithful to it, from remembering who she had been, from never defiling her memory by dwelling on the prurient or the merely scandalous.

As I set down the roses, I saw at once that the coffin-sized rectangle of earth reaching out below Alex's headstone was covered with what I estimated to be perhaps a two-week growth of weeds. Even though I'd half-expected this (I'd heard rumours that her remains would be exhumed, although I can't remember from where), I was abruptly sobered, thinking, *They really mean it; they really mean to find her murderer at last*, which I had not fully believed until I saw this concrete evidence of it, because when I'd tried to determine what had happened, at every turn I had met a frustrating wall of obfuscation, of refusal, of continued secrecy. Now I felt also something that might have been fear at my own audacity, as well as an unexpected shock that my seemingly fruitless efforts might have, by chain effects, caused this to happen, "this" being that her last resting place had been defiled, and for this outrage, I might be ultimately responsible.

I was shaken enough, confused by all the ideas tumbling through my head, that when I left her grave, intending also to visit my parents' graves and my sister's, I'd been unable to find them, and after ten minutes of driving in circles around the large cemetery and seeming to be farther from wherever I'd thought I was than when I began, I abandoned the hunt and drove, uncertainly, away.

Hours later, I realized that in that meticulously kept, beautiful old cemetery, a patch of weeds would be allowed to stay only if the coffin had been taken away and was expected to be soon returned. I had been confused and dismayed enough not to have thought through what I was seeing. Now I was jolted by the conscious realization that I had left my roses on a rectangle of earth containing nothing but insects, the unsprung seeds of grass and weeds, and crumbling earth. Alex's remains hadn't even been there.

It took me weeks to get beyond the fact of that patch of weeds, and my casual, unexamined assumptions as to the reason, to give the purpose of the exhumation more thought. I knew that there had been marvellous advances in DNA technology, and the newest advance I had heard of would make practically anything possible, it seemed to unscientific me. That is, the advance called "low copy DNA," by which a fragment as small as a single cell can be endlessly, exactly, replicated so that what previously would have been too small a sample to be tested could now be copied until there was enough to identify. I knew that previous attempts had been made. Later I would wonder, provided the thirty hair samples of the television documentary and the one hundred hair samples of the RCMP lab report were one and the same, if the larger swatch had diminished as, over the years, hairs were sent off for testing—and had failed because there wasn't enough material, or the material had deteriorated too much.

It had been reported in the *Star Phoenix*, too, that before Alex's mother had died, a sample had been taken from her, although the reason—I think to collect mitochondrial DNA that would match Alex's—had been kept from her. And I remembered again that I'd been informed that in the nineties the then police chief had told reporters that he hoped to have a DNA profile of the killer soon, although nothing further had been reported on that front.

224 The Girl in Saskatoon

I went back to the January 2004 taped documentary *Death of a Beauty Queen*. The police officer then investigating Alex's file had made a comment about this, and I wanted to review it.

"You have DNA," the interviewer says, more a question than a statement. The officer replies, "We're working on developing a profile from exhibits that indicate to us that there is possibly DNA there. We rely on the forensic lab people to tell us yes, we have a profile for you."

I'm not sure whether the officer is saying yes, or no. He says that they are working on it. On what? "We're working on developing a profile," which means that there is DNA there, although the last part of the sentence, "possibly," contradicts the first part. And yet, you wouldn't work on developing a profile until you had DNA to do it with. The second sentence says what we already know, that it takes forensic lab people to develop the profile from the DNA material. Does his reply actually mean: We have DNA, we are waiting for a profile to be developed? I think it does.

But the grave was disturbed in August 2004, nearly a year after that interview had been conducted, and eight months after the airing of *Death of a Beauty Queen*. The lab must have declared that it needed more material, or different material, in order to verify its first findings, or because even with the new technology the material they had was too deteriorated to be useful. (The documentary also mentions "swabs" taken, presumably at the autopsy, although there is no mention of swabs on the 1962 RCMP lab report, or the autopsy report, nor what they are swabs of, but I am guessing they are of the material in Alex's "vaginal vault," although the pathologist notes that her fingernails are perfectly groomed and short, except for her thumbnails, which were long—I am thinking, because she played the acoustic guitar—maybe swabs were used to take out the material found under them.)

DNA empties the crime of its passion, its mystery, its motivations, of reports, rumour, speculation, suspicion. DNA—a swab, a hair, a particle of skin. All of it, everything, comes down to this: a laboratory, a latex-gloved scientist, a microscope, a computer, DNA samples. Forty-some years of questioning and remembering, rendered down to this still, quiet moment, when the scientist sees the two DNA patterns that match.

One night Alex went for a walk, she stayed at the weir until dark waiting for someone who probably didn't come. Someone else came, a man who had been stalking her, and he was watching her the whole time she sat gazing at the river, waiting for it to grow dark, waiting for everyone else to leave, afraid to grapple with her on the apron for fear they might both tumble into the river, which at that place with water pouring over the fish ladder was dangerous, waiting for Alex to rise and start for home.

At last she did. She walked to the top of the concrete apron and turned right, going under the bridge, where he stepped out of the shadows and grabbed her and held her fast, while she resisted, pushing him away, and he began to drag her down to that little island of trees and she tried to escape from him, but he wouldn't let go of her, and near the trees, struggling and failing to pull away, she began screaming. Infuriated, maybe even a bit scared, to stop her noise he punched her in the face as hard as he could, smashing her nose and blackening her eye, and because she was unable to breathe through her nose now, and stunned with pain and shock and terror, too, it was easy for him to throw her to the ground—perhaps she banged her head on concrete debris or on a rock as she fell—and he fell on top of her, trying to pin her down, and she roused herself to try to fight him off. Now she was seeing that she might die here, in this ghastly way—she was seeing all her dreams for her wonderful future, all the promises she read in the signs around her about what magic lay in the world for her, and how far she had to go and how much she would see and do and become—and he, this evil thing on top of her determined to take it all away, to end everything. So she fought him with every ounce of strength she had, tearing hair from his head, and raking skin from his face and neck, and when she wouldn't stop, he grew beyond himself and his own desire, or his own fury, and he grasped her by the shoulders or her head and smashed her head as hard as he could against whatever it was that lay there, rocks, concrete debris, and she fell unconscious. Hastily he tore apart her clothing, he pushed her legs up and apart, he raped her, and then, satisfied, panting, he drew back, and as the tumult slowly stilled, as the thunder in his head dimmed, he held still to listen to the city night, hearing nothing that would tell him someone was near and about to set off an alarm, knowing now, himself, what he had done, and that she knew him, or had seen his face. Or maybe that didn't matter at all to him, maybe his plan had always been to kill her if he had to. But perhaps she was already dead? No, he could feel her chest still moving, or maybe he put his ear to her mouth and felt the warm, moisture-laden breath—her nose smashed, she could breathe only through her mouth and maybe that was noisy—maybe he could hear her laboured, shallow, quick breath. Then, he thought, *She will die soon*—and more—in a still moment of pure evil he thought: *I can make sure of that.* And he picked up a piece of concrete debris and set it carefully on her chest, maybe thinking that it would crush that last breath out of her, or else that even if she should regain consciousness she would be too weak to lift it off herself or to roll away from it. And then he threw dirt on her, he buried her, there, still alive, in the moonlight, among the trees, beside the river.

By Alex's abrupt, savage end, the Wiwcharuks were brought to the edge of a chasm—the darkness of our deaths, the absolute loneliness of them—and have stood, in shock and horror, teetering on its brink ever since. As Marie says at the end of her documentary interview, in a voice that drops to a near-whisper in her effort to control her emotion after all these years of thinking, wondering, remembering, moving through rage and unbearable sorrow and back again, "I keep thinking . . . When . . . do you . . . forget?"

## Chapter Ten
## Fern Creek

It is true that you can only make sense of the present if you know the past, if you know how you got from there to here, that we need the past to keep us from forgetting who we are, where our souls reside, and of what they are truly made. And so, I have gone backwards in this book to all our beginnings in Saskatchewan, during the war, and on the land, where Alex and I began. But for many years, since I came down here to the far southwest of the province to live, when people asked me where I came from, I would say, after a hesitation and without any certainty in my voice, as if I myself wasn't sure, "From Saskatoon." And then I would be pleased at having found an answer to that oft-repeated, ages-old question, an answer that sounded plausible and that satisfied people, so that they didn't take a step closer to me, peer into my face, and say, "But, I mean, really: Where are you from?" although at first I half-expected them to.

But that was never their realization, it was always my own, that though I could reasonably say that Saskatoon was my hometown, my true feeling was that I hadn't such a thing as a hometown, and this contradiction made me uncomfortable. The real place I had come from was always there, hovering in the back of my mind like a dark cloud about to spill rain, and I always had a sense of the impossibility of explaining what that place meant in my life, and how it had shaped me, and thus, maybe, deserved to be called home.

So when my sixtieth birthday was approaching, the gift I asked for was to return to the place from which I had come. This meant going to the homesteads north of Garrick, along the edge of the boreal forest, my grandparents' and my parents', to which I was brought after my birth. It was not just that if I returned there I might find a better answer to the question of where I had come from, but also that I needed to see the past for myself, as a grown-up, to see the scenes of my child-hood, and that out of this I might, also, find a more satisfactory answer to that question about where my true home was. So one very hot day in late August, my husband and I set out on the three-hundred-mile drive north, in order that I would be at the places of my earliest memories of life, on the very day of my sixtieth birthday. We stayed overnight in a motel in the nearest big town, and on the morning of my birthday, we set out to find the homestead sites.

All day, as we drove, or walked—as we had to do to reach my grandparents' homestead site, there being no roads in—I kept looking for something; I thought that I might catch some wisp of scent that would bring back to me, full blown, my own past and my family's past; that perhaps I would hear a sound, a bird singing in the grass or calling from the forest, or the rumble of antique farm machinery, that would do it. Or I would see a sawmill at work, the master saw whining its way through pine or spruce, maple or poplar, growling furiously as it chewed up knots, spitting bark and splinters, the sunlight paled through dust as the pile of sawdust below the machine grew, and I would be transported to my childhood world.

Maybe I would see a rusted and flattened blue granite basin lying in the grass, one that I remembered washing my face in nearly sixty years before—the one in a black-and-white snapshot I have in which I sit in bright sunshine, a year-old child, fat and grinning innocently, the basin resting on a wide tree stump in front of our log house. It is the basin, I think, in which around that time a sibling tried to drown me, the sibling says, and about which I recall only my mother and father, some years later, laughing in a faintly astonished, faintly shamed way. Laughing, probably, because it was the only way they knew how to deal with such a thing, one that they didn't dare to examine too closely. I hoped something would call up a picture, pure and true—*visceral* in its immediacy—of the past I needed to reclaim.

I wanted to see this northern world as it had been when I was a small child, when there were no built-up roads, and no frame buildings or sheds sheeted over with brightly coloured tin, and so, when we happened to pass a sandy trail with grass growing raggedly on its verges, I asked my husband to turn. Up we went on it, passing a spot where the sand was so deep we could see that someone had recently been stuck in it, until

we reached a stand of four or five thirty-foot-high, resplend-
ent white spruces in the corner of a plowed farmer's field. I
got out and looked around, and then, tentatively, pressed my
palms to the bark of their sturdy trunks, waiting for something
that never came. After that, we searched out the decaying, col-
lapsing log houses—one of them had been a school, although
I'd never attended it—from my pioneer past. They stood in
hip-high grass, holes rubbed in their roofs by tree branches,
their doors long gone, the boards once nailed over their windows to keep out birds and animals, hanging crookedly by
one fastening. Their builders were gone, or dead, and I didn't
remember them anyway.

We visited an old lady who, we'd been assured, had been
our neighbour, who said she had come as a young woman from
the great distance then of fifty miles away to be my mother's
"hired girl." A year later she left to marry, spending the rest
of her life five miles down the road from the kitchen where
she and my mother had laboured together in the sweltering,
insect-ridden summer heat, and the frigid, snow-swamped
winters. She made my husband and me lunch, served on a
hand-embroidered tablecloth she said my grandmother had
given her as a wedding present.

When eventually we found my grandparents' homestead site,
I was only half-surprised, given the woman my grandmother
had been, to find how beautiful it was. The house, now gone,
had been set on a grassy knoll facing southeast; at its base there
was a stream named by my grandmother Fern Creek, which ran
parallel to the house and to the row of tall, blue-green spruces

with their reddish bark that my grandfather had planted, one for each grandchild, in front of it. How green everything was, how lush the grass sprinkled with pink wild roses, and yellow, white, and blue wildflowers, how dense with leaves the poplars and the ashes. The creek splashed softly over flattened grass and small stones; it was easy to jump across it, although I remembered from family stories that for weeks in spring the stream swelled until it was too deep and swift to cross.

Only about a half-mile behind where the house and barn once would have been, the farmer who was showing us around told us about the time, having driven out there to burn some garbage in my grandparents' cellar depression, he had come upon four bears playing in the grass. Even though he had been here all his life, the four bears seemed to surprise and delight him. North of the spot where the four bears tumbled in the grass is still, as it was when I was a newborn, nothing but trees and more trees, until, many miles to the north, the barrenlands begin, and the tundra, and then the arctic. There were no roads going north from there and there still are none. There was, likewise, no road leading south from the homestead to civilization, but the trail my grandparents took that would lead them a mile south to our family's house was still visible as wagonwheel depressions overgrown with thick grass of the brightest green, and running through a now-permanent clearing in the forest. All day I searched the wall of trees, quiescent in the humidity-laden heat, the lush green grass we walked through, the rutted, sandy road we drove along, the few tall spruces at its end.

At last we found the site of my first home. We saw at once that the owner had torn down what was left of it. He had hauled away the rotting logs, the scarred wooden window-frames, the misshapen door I'd seen as background in the black-and-white snapshots. There was only a small pile of decayed and blackened wood, in front of a clump of trees that was all that was left of the forest that had been cleared away around it, and I remembered how one morning we'd wakened to see two bears making themselves at home in the grassy clearing around our settler's shack, and how my father, in his pyjamas, had clapped his hands over his head loudly to scare them away.

But I stared at the spot where I had spent the first few years of my life. I looked especially at the trees—birches, poplars, willows—that grew around the hollow where our log house had been, and down into a darkly gleaming pond beside it, the existence of which I had no recollection at all. I gazed into the impenetrable, still surface of the water, in which I saw now, a lush, golden-green willow grew, its unseen roots clinging to the rich soil far below.

I saw then that this was the true place of my beginnings— this forest, this grass, these ruined settlers' homes. I was surprised to feel a kind of satisfaction at the thought, as if I'd finally banished some doubt I'd held about having origins, that I had come from nowhere, had wakened one morning, full-blown, in Saskatoon, although that one year when I was a west-side kid, stunned by the roughness of the city, by its underlife, and by its possibilities, was indeed a true and vital awakening. But that dim, tumultuous past in the northern forest, those sometimes-brilliant mental pictures of it, those worn stories of our family life there, all of this tinged with sadness and with wonder—now they settled quietly into place. It was all so long ago, I thought, and although I will never deny this place, it was in Saskatoon that I grew into consciousness, that I began, so slowly, over the years, to make my life my own.

Then I knew that if I were to properly tell Alex's story, I would have to go to the place from which she had come. For more than thirty years I've lived on the west side of the province and down by the American border, while Alex's home village, Endeavour, is on the opposite side and more than a hundred miles north. It would be a long trip, but on my way I would stop to talk to anyone I could find who had known her in Yorkton when she'd attended nursing school there. I was going alone, my husband would be haying—and being a fifties girl and a married woman most of the years since I was twenty-one, I was both a little scared and excited at the prospect of taking charge of my own thousand-mile-plus trip.

I had booked into a bed-and-breakfast at Yorkton, a small city where, despite having spent nearly all my life in Saskatchewan, I had never been, and in conversation with the owners—one more time I wondered what Alex had had to do with my choice, this time of where I would stay—we discovered that he had known Alex very well, used to double date with her and their respective dates when Alex was a vivacious, strikingly pretty, young nursing student. It took my breath away, that coincidence.

The morning after my evening's conversation with the

owner of the Yorkton B & B, I rose early and set out north for Endeavour. The day was clear and bright and warm and the road good, and I felt exhilarated. I could feel my car's easy power under my foot as if it, too, couldn't wait to get to Alex's hometown. It took me almost an hour and a half, partly because I kept slowing down to make notes (which I would never use), and to stare at crops and trees and farmhouses and the villages and towns I passed along the way. But at last I arrived, and as I drove through Alex's home village, my impression was of a clean, bright place, well-manicured up to the edge of the forest, which, in its blue-green, dangerous, and beautifully wild way, pressed in on three sides.

Endeavour's population was listed at 154, although only nine years earlier, in 1996, it had twenty more people (a drop of twelve percent). Like all Western Canadian villages, it had a small grocery store, a hotel and bar (advertising Wing Night, that day I drove in), a post office, and a liquor store located in the same building, a town office open only on Fridays, a couple of churches, one Orthodox and one Protestant, and a town hall. It was the frame hall that caught my eye: Its name, in large letters above the double front doors, was written only in Cyrillic, with a logo above it which I recognized as two stylized birds with a burning candle between them. Later, I was told that the sign reads, *Ukrainian National Home of Taras Shevchenko*.

Having been raised in Saskatchewan among Ukrainian people, I knew in a vague way who Shevchenko was, but in 2005 to find his name still up, and in Ukrainian—well, I thought I'd better do some research. Taras Shevchenko (1814–1861) I found out, was born a serf, but because he was so gifted he was taught to read and write, and others eventually purchased his freedom and helped him to become educated. He moved to St. Petersburg where he studied, painted, and began to write poetry. But what would make this tiny village in a faraway country, all these years later, commemorate his name is that he wrote in Ukrainian, not in Russian or Polish, and by doing so, he created not only the Ukrainian language—considered up to then to be merely a dialect of Russian, and unworthy of literature—but also gave full voice to Ukrainian nationalism. Persecuted by the czar, he was only forty-seven when he died, but the very strong sense Ukrainians have of who they are, and of their rightful place in history, is mostly attributed to Shevchenko, who now has the status of Ukrainian national poet. His name on the community hall, and in Ukrainian, speaks volumes about the Ukrainian-Canadian community into which Alex was born.

I drove up and down the few streets and studied the twenty or so frame houses on them. Then, I began to follow the narrow trail-like roads into the forest, not knowing what I would find, but there I discovered more small frame houses, which were, except for their neatly cleared, good-sized yards, set solidly in forest. I thought at first there were perhaps twenty houses in the village, but after following roads I saw leading into the bush, I realized there were more likely as many as fifty. Mostly the houses were well-maintained bungalows of the sort you see rows and rows of in city suburbs, but nothing very large or extravagant; these were either frugal people, or there is, as people had told me, little wealth in the area.

I wanted to find the farmstead where Alex had grown up, and Marie had told me, more or less, its coordinates. I found the right road, and drove very slowly up and down it, staring at the small fields, some cropped, some in summer-fallow, some overgrown with thick, wild green grass, and all framed by forest. There were rotting log buildings in places, well back of the road, and ancient barbed-wire fences, and birds, and the occasional wild animal—a bushy-tailed red fox, a white-tail doe—but no home place that I recognized from the photos Alex's sister Ann had sent me. And anyway, Ann had told me, their original home (of logs, like mine had been) was destroyed by fire, the bane of homesteaders in the early days, in which they'd lost a sewing machine, a big floor-model radio, and other precious items.

I was overwhelmed by the great natural beauty of the place, and of the lushness of the growth, by the vistas of thick blue-green forest undulating for miles, gently, toward the distant horizon. Even today, even knowing what no Saskatchewan person can fail to know about the history of the place—the cruel displacement of the Aboriginal peoples, the often desperate hardship of settle-ment—I was overcome by this stunning, wild beauty. Knowing that Alex knew no other landscape until she was fifteen, I could only wonder how it might have forged her soul, her definition of beauty, her longings for the place she called home. And I imag-ined, too, that when she let her mind roam free, as I have thought she did that night, sitting alone in the moonlight on the weir's concrete apron as the wide South Saskatchewan flowed in its near-silent, power-filled way past her, these were the scenes that floated, dreamlike, behind her eyes. And where were her guardian angels that night? Where, oh where, I wondered, was the warning system to tell her to go home before it grew dark, while there were still people around?

As I drove back westward, to my country home, past field after field where crops ripened in the high heat of late summer, I could not stop thinking about Alex, how beautiful she was at twenty, and twenty-two and -three, and how I had never noticed that potential in her features when we were both small, dark, plump high school girls. Then I realized something that had been bothering me for a long time without ever coming squarely into my conscious mind. It was why anyone—any man—would punch this beauty queen, the very fact that made her so desirable, directly in the face.

I didn't want to think about it, because in doing my interviewing I had spoken to a number of men who remembered her and who sounded as if they were still weak in the knees at the memory of how pretty she was, and the longing, combined with regret, and pity, too, in their voices—as well as something I began to interpret as a sort of diffuse shame—never failed to shock me. These were men who fell into silence at her memory; I felt I could see them quietly accepting that such beauty was beyond them. Her memory called up their manhood in much more than the sexual sense, not just as designated protectors of womanhood, either, but in some dim and distant way, as making a connection with the power and ineffable beauty of the feminine.

The killer chose Alex; whether he knew her personally or not, she was not a random choice. The neighbourhood was full of attractive young women, many of them nurses at the nearby hospital, and a large number lived in the student nurses' residence next door to the hospital, none as pretty as Alex. But Alex was also "famous," in that she'd been in the newspapers three times as a beauty contest winner or runner-up, and probably on television, too, and men were attracted to her the instant they saw her. Her desirability was such that she never lacked for male company. If she was stalked, then she was stalked for her beauty. It might have been any one of us raped, beaten, and murdered that night, but it was not. In the end, I think it was her beauty that got her killed.

Travelling in Mexico one winter, friends took us to visit the artisans' shops and studios in Tlaquepaque outside Guadalajara. There I saw and bought a wooden bas-relief of Mary, but the Mexican Mary, the Virgin of Guadaloupe, the one of the story about the pious Mexican boy, now San Juan de Dios, for whom she performed a miracle. In this rendering, she is surrounded by what appear to be rays of light, but which are meant to represent the stripes of Juan's serape, at her feet are two black horns, the horns of the moon, and usually there is also a cherub at her feet, I suppose to represent her son, the Christ child. The base of mine is dark blue and sprinkled with painted-on gold stars, her robe is red, decorated with gold designs, her cape is green and covered with stars, she wears a golden crown. Vivid and rich-looking, this depiction represents something much greater and of longer standing, something much more universal about womanhood, something I can relate to as a female, a woman, than the Mary I learned about as a child. And so, she stands in my office, gazing out boldly, not submissively, smiling. It isn't much, it occurs to me, but it will have to do for wisdom about the world.

There is one more detail I have omitted (there are others, but of less weight): The children who discovered Alex's body did so because they saw her hand lifted up through the sand of her grave. I thought, in the way that one does, without thinking, that this must have been caused by rigor mortis, and that it was of no particular significance. But as I thought and thought about her death, and consulted an expert on that phenomenon, I began to think that instead, when she was still living, after the killer had left her there to die, she had lifted her hand through the dirt of her grave in an effort to free herself, in an effort to cry for help, and then she had died, her hand raised in that last anguished and pathetic gesture. If she had not done that, how long would it have been before she was found? Would she ever have been found?

After I'd carried my roses to Alex's grave that summer day, only to find that it had been disturbed, and I'd driven away in confusion, I had a second visit to make. I'd gotten word that after a fight—citizens against city hall and the developers—the high school that Alex and I had attended, Tech, was being torn down, and I wanted to see it one last time. But I'd had to put off my trip to the city for one reason or another several times, so that by the time I got there, and walked in toward it the way I always had, through the parking lot, past the Canadian Legion, and into the alley to the door we were required to use, I saw at once that most of the school's three storeys of muted gold bricks had been reduced to an enormous pile of rubble and the pile was surrounded by a high, chain link fence well-posted with warning signs. The last time I'd been on that spot in 1997, I think, garbage cans had stood at the door, but this time, although the door—a fine French door, its frame now painted a glutinous yellow—was still standing and on its hinges, whatever the hinges had been attached to was lost in the heap of broken chunks of grey cement, of bricks tossed this way and that, some single, some still welded together by chipped and pitted mortar.

Someone, for privacy, I suppose, had once pasted newspaper behind the door's glass; it had yellowed and been water-stained, but despite every pane of glass being smashed, I saw that the newspaper, bizarrely, was still intact. Mr. McPherson's social studies classroom—I'd last been in it when I did my interview with *the fifth estate*—Mr. Harm's literature classroom, the library where I'd spent more and more of my time as the years passed toward graduation and where Alex and I sometimes attended drama practice, the room where Miss Hagerman taught typing and business practice, Mr. Chan's drafting room, even—or especially—Ernie Lindner's art room, where he had reigned from 1936 to 1962, all destroyed, gone, smashed into that tower of debris. And the debris sitting on top of what had been our combination gymnasium and auditorium where every Friday we jived our way through lunch hour at dance practice.

A hard-hatted workman wearing a bright orange vest was sitting in the shade on a lawn chair across the alley on my right, and I feared he might rise at any moment to chase me away, so I kept walking away from him, to my left, purposefully, down the alley toward the front of the building. But the high chain-link fence extended half a city block out in front of the ruins, enclosing the trees and lawn as well, and when I walked farther, trying to circle the school, thinking to approach it more closely through the parking lot, I saw that it was fenced too, right up to the edge of the river that now flowed past a pile of ruins. The only way to get near would be to come back in the night and climb the fence. (Or to row up the river in the darkness and climb the bank.)

Even though the small-gauge mesh of the fence obscured the view, I could see that all that was left standing was the central section of the front facade, the wide front steps of the main entrance, above them the ornate double wooden doors, glassless now and sheeted on the inside with unpainted plywood, with the still intact and attached darkened bronze canopy over it, and above it, a tall panel of moulded, decorative cement, rising to the second storey. The large, once-graceful, many-paned windows on each side of the door were now gaping holes, the one on the right still with its interior framing, but no glass, and the frame itself misshapen, the upper right corner broken and the cracked brick around it bulging dangerously outward. The tall, old maples and elms in front of the building hid most of where the third storey had been, so that there was only a dark silhouette protruding jaggedly into the hot August sky.

It was as if I were surrounded by those teenagers who'd gone to school there with me, now sober adults, perhaps still living—although I doubted it—in the small, frame houses set close together on tiny lots on the city's west side. More likely, the older ones from the thirties dead now, and those closer to my age, given how the world has changed, scattered around the continents, or at the very least, living in pleasant, middle-class houses in Nutana, or in the new subdivisions that Alex had never seen, farther to the east, or to the north, beyond the place where she'd been killed, and beyond her grave in Wood-lawn. It was as if all of them were there with me, viewing the remains of our old school, and mourning them, mourn-ing our youth, thinking, too, of the friends lost to history, the boy-and-girl friends we'd thought we loved, or maybe really did, married to someone else for thirty or more years, liv-ing elsewhere—in the Okanagan, in southwestern Ontario, on "the Island," meaning Vancouver Island—and gone forever from our lives.

In fact, despite now living five hours away, I had been peripherally involved in the organized movement to save the school and to turn it into a complex of facilities that the people of the city could enjoy—a people's market, a theatre, meeting rooms, a mothering centre, a children's museum, a restaurant. Most recently, our old school had been the Gathercole Centre when Saskatoon's board of education made it its headquarters, Gathercole having once been the superintendent of educa-tion. (This was after it had been for a few years a special school called Riverside Collegiate.) Closed down when the Board

of Education had given up its attempt to build a new building and had moved into the old Eaton's building a few blocks
away (which had since 1973 or so been the Army and Navy
store), in its most recent incarnation our school had been a set
for an American television comedy, *Body and Soul*, sometimes
directed and produced by Anson Williams, who had been
"Potsie" of the popular television show *Happy Days* (set, ironically, in the fifties). *Body and Soul* had turned the interior of
our school into a hospital, but for its exterior, used the newly
built white and silver City Hospital—Alex had worked in the
old red-brick City Hospital—with its super-modern styling.
My son, married and a father, had become an actor and had
had a small, recurring role in the few episodes shot of *Body and
Soul*; that he had worked inside his parents' old high school
made me marvel once again at life's coincidences, and also at
how intertwined all our lives are.

Two workmen passed by me going down the alley, staring
at me as they went. A moment later, they came back again, and
because they seemed so interested in me, I said, pointing at the
rubble as if I were throwing something, "This used to be my
high school."

One of them said, "Would you like a brick?" Taken by surprise, I hesitated—*Why would I want a brick?*—then said, dubi-
ously, "Yes, okay, sure." He made his way through a break in the
fence, climbed onto the pile, and asked me, "Which one?" *Imagine
him asking me which one*, I thought. It was all such a peculiar marvel, the school that had stood there for seventy-three years now
demolished, unsentimental me standing here mourning it, and

some inextricable and yet unexplained connection between this demolition and Alex and her terrible story bedevilling me. But, having consented, I helped him pick a single brick, one without a scratch or a chip, and clean of mortar. I put it in my bag, and walked slowly away to my car.

I had one more stop to make before I turned and headed toward my home. Once again, as I had that hot day in May a few years ago, the day I realized how, despite everything, I loved this city, I left the site of the school and drove down Spadina Crescent north to the weir, where I pulled into the parking lot and shut off the motor. Pelicans were feeding down below, their great orange beaks poking holes in the sky and water. They hadn't been there when Alex died, but now they come every year, and their extravagant forms are one of the sights that draw people to this place.

Asphalt has been poured, and the parking lot where I sat is arranged now so that one row of cars may park side by side, noses pointed to the water. The fence is solid brown iron now, and if you go to it and peer down between the fence and the water's edge, you see that the concrete apron where Alex sat that night is still there, seamed with cracks now, through which green grass and weeds poke their bright heads. Fishing is no longer allowed; no one is allowed to go down onto the apron anymore, and the fence makes it nearly impossible anyway. Far to the left, about a tenth of a mile from the centre of the old apron, the high iron railway bridge has a new, many levelled set of firm, wide steps leading onto it, which invite walkers, and at ground level there are picnic tables and benches and a walking path. The spot on the far side of the bridge where Alex's body was found cannot be identified now. Somewhere in that greenery above the water she died, and was buried, and then found. There is no way at all for a stranger to know that this is where a beautiful young woman had her life taken from her.

We are made of stories, it is said; without stories, we don't exist at all: that time when everybody thought the old "tin bridge" was about to go out in the spring breakup; or when in a sudden downpour the underpass filled with water and a woman's car stalled and her electric doors and windows wouldn't open and she drowned; or the time the creamery barn caught fire and thirty horses died; or that strange, scruffy, wild-looking man who rode a bike everywhere for years and years and then one day was gone; or how we all got out of bed one frosty Saturday morning each year and walked down to the civic arena so that we could cheer the east-west elementary school hockey game; or how the big Friday night date used to be to go to a movie at the Capitol Theatre or the old Tivoli. Or that young, beauty-queen-nurse who was murdered and they never caught her killer. These are stories that belong to all of us and that weave us together, give us our sense of belonging, and our sense of home. That there is no separating the city story from the individual story is something I did not know, twenty years ago when I dreamt that dream about the Ukrainian Hall on the west side of Saskatoon, and my diary in it, under glass.

Perhaps that dream, where all this began for me, had an imperative hidden from me: that one day I would hear about the other diary, the one written by Alex that was burned, and the day that I realized there were two diaries—today, as I write these words—I would feel a completion of the circle of story about two small, quiet, country girls from meagre circumstances who went to the city and, despite the things that happened to them there, and the one dead, and the other far away, never really left it again. And I would feel once again, how we, although mere acquaintances and never close friends, had been linked by circumstance and history, and by memory. As if destiny had decided what would happen: she would die a terrible death and receive no justice, and I would be a writer and try to write her story into permanency, whether or not her killer was ever caught. That, I think, is the prophecy of my dream of twenty years ago and of the two diaries which have become one, melding two girls' lives in story.

The brick I took that day from the pile of rubble that had been our school sits on my desk. In this early morning light, the sky cloudy, it is oddly transformed and faded, the sharp edges gone, the harshness smoothed. Finely and shallowly ribbed on three sides in a muted grey, up close I see that what I have called yellow is a rich cream, and yet most of the edge that would be visible in a building has been discoloured, or more likely, designed to change in the firing to a warm shade somewhere between peach and pink. A work of art was this brick, and I wondered if that was why it broke our hearts to see the building reduced to trash by wrecking ball and bulldozer. I cherish that brick as a representative of our precious youth, Alex's and mine, when we traipsed every day to that big, yellow-gold building on the riverbank that stood under the shade of the maples and elms, where we dreamed our dreams of a future full of love, adventure, and happiness, and the whole world seemed to be waiting to embrace us.

# Epilogue

A couple of years ago at a retreat-resort centre, I had the good luck, by virtue of standing next to him in the line, to have an intimate breakfast with a famous Zen monk. He said to me, during our conversation, "I always wanted to be a poet." "Oh?" I said, and we went on to talk a bit about the writerly impulse. But when he had said that, unexpectedly, as if from some source other than myself, so that I was partly stunned by it even as we spoke quietly together about other things, what had popped into my head had been, *I always wanted to be alive.*

I had hoped that this book would end with the name of Alex's killer, and the news of his capture and incarceration, and with all the details of that night, the motives, the passion laid bare at last. So, in late 2006, just as I had finished writing this story, I was thrilled when something happened that I thought would at last make it possible for me to say the killer's name. I received a letter from the daughter of the sixteen-year-old boy who had been fishing at the weir that night, Billy McGaffin, who had been hypnotized by Dr. Brand and who had said under hypnosis that he had seen two cars there that night.

His daughter told me that her father—long divorced from her mother—had died in 1998 in Manitoba, but even more startling to one who had read every syllable printed on the subject of that night, she said that her father's younger brother, then twelve years old, had been with him at the weir that fateful night. I had wondered (and concluded that it was a mistake) why the CBC documentary had shown five boys at the weir when I'd thought that there was one boy—Billy—fishing on Alex's right, and the two boys who'd been behind her, gazing longingly down at her, and who, one of them had told me, didn't even know until the police told them, that the first boy was from their class at school.

But Angela's uncle, when she asked him to tell her about her father being implicated in a murder, told her that the police had continued to visit him, asking him questions over and over again about that night, and about his older brother's actions. It seems obvious that the police had always suspected Billy. I remember that at one point in my questioning, I had wondered seriously if the police had considered her father as a suspect, but because he was so young, and because there was no hint in the newspapers or from any other of my sources that he had been anything but a valued witness, I had dismissed that idea. That he was a redhead was always mentioned, though, which should have told me something, but in my inexperience, failed to put me on the alert. I knew now, having discovered it late in this process, that that had to be because red or reddish hair had been discovered on Alex's body or clothing (although when I finally saw the RCMP lab report, I could find no mention of such hair). The 2004 CBC documentary, too, had described him as a suspect at first, but said that under hypnosis he had "all but cleared himself"—and I had taken that as the final word.

His daughter went on to write that, "Along with my mom & brother, I gave a DNA sample in the summer of 2004." (That was the same summer that I visited Alex's grave with my bouquet of deep red roses, and discovered that her remains had been disturbed.) She also wrote that since they had given their DNA samples, two years or so earlier, they had heard not a word from the police. But, she explained, the Saskatoon police officer who had taken her family's samples had told her that they were taking those of many suspicious people and contacts, and that when all were gathered, they would send them together to a certain lab for testing. She had written that she guessed that that would take a long time.

I called her by phone as soon as I had read and reread her letter, but she had gone away for the weekend, her phone wasn't working properly either, and it was three endless days before I heard from her. When we finally spoke, she told me that until the time of the DNA sample, she and her brother had known nothing at all about the cloud of suspicion that had been hanging over their father ever since that night in 1962, and she doubts that her mother knew either. She was thoroughly shocked, she said, and it took her a while to get a grip on this information and to begin to think about it in a rational way, and then she had wanted to know more about that night, she had wanted to know everything.

She had been living in England, she said, when a friend who had seen the documentary, *Death of a Beauty Queen*, sent her a copy of the videotape. Unfortunately, the tape was damaged and she had been able to recover only the soundtrack, not the picture. She said she'd wanted to phone me from the moment she heard the tape and recovered from the shock of discovering that her own father had been—still was—a murder suspect, but had thought that I would think she was simply crazy. But finally she had decided to take the risk and write to me. I said that I would make a copy of the tape and try sending it to her again.

At first, on hearing this news from the suspect's daughter, I was merely excited, feeling that at last I had a grip on the missing piece of the mystery. And yet, I told myself, I'd always known there were suspects, I just didn't know who they were. Surely, knowing now who one of them was didn't change anything. But by the morning after Angela and I had finally had our long, excited conversation—she was dying for details about the story, and I was dying to know about her father—I was beginning to feel quite differently about this new development. I decided to view the documentary one more time.

It showed five boys, and I could, even now, only account for four who had been there that night, and I thought that if Billy had been pursued by the police until his death, and his brother's presence had been kept a forty-four year secret, then two of the three remaining boys were probably on the suspect list too. Although I had the name of one, I had never even tried to talk to him, and I had no idea who the fifth boy was (if, indeed, there had been a fifth boy). The man who had been the third boy had called me and we had talked several times; he said he'd never been contacted by the police since the day he'd gone to the station to tell them he'd seen Alex that night, nor had he been asked for his DNA. I reasoned that if he was not a suspect, then the friend who'd been with him that night probably never was either—this, I supposed, was because neither of them was a redhead. But who, then, was that other figure?

I'd had a long, sleepless night, trying to figure out where the information from Angela fit into my book, if it fit at all, or if it was just another story to add to the many stories I'd already recounted. I woke depressed when I should have been tense with excitement: I should have been holding all my emotions in abeyance as I waited for the news of the DNA results. But instead, as the morning wore on I grew more depressed, until I was unable to write, and eventually found myself near tears. Partly because now I had more material to use and would have to go back and figure out if it changed everything or it changed nothing or somewhere in between, and already this book had exhausted me. I had said to my editor, *This book will be the death of me*; I didn't know if I would be able to find the stamina, or even more lethally to such an effort, the desire to revise it yet another time.

As the morning wore on, however, I knew my reaction to be something more profound than mere exhaustion at the possibility of having to do yet another tinkering with my book, yet I could not quite divine what it was. I saw now that I had been deceived, one way or another, over and over again, deceived by omission, mostly, and by people I had believed in absolutely, all that long time ago, believing in their integrity, and in their desire to find justice for Alex. And now I saw that everybody had turf to protect, everybody had kept secrets; they had kept secrets from each other, and from me, and most of all, I was beginning to think, from themselves. For a while I thought that this had to be the source of my deep unease, and I thought that sooner or later I would just get over it.

It was only a week or so later that Angela sent me a copy of the e-mail her family had received from a Saskatoon police officer, which stated, to her family's huge relief, that the comparison of DNA samples had fully and completely exonerated her father. I was not exactly surprised, and I was truly happy for Billy McGaffin's family, who by then had suffered over this possibility for a long time, had had their lives turned upside down by it, had had to rethink everything they knew about their father and their mutual past. How very hard that must have been. It made no difference to my book that he was not the killer; I had tried to write it about something other than who the killer was. But still, I remained deeply troubled by this whole development, and I could not put my finger on the reason.

I told myself glumly that despite this interlude of high drama, I was back where I had started, meaning that I was back at the moment before I tore open Angela's letter and read the startling news. But now I realized that I could never go back to where I had been, not to that moment when my book was nearly finished and I didn't know the names of any of the suspects, and I certainly couldn't go back to however many years ago, when I started this long search. It all had taken too much out of me, it had shown me too much about my home, this place so far from the capitals of the world, and by their standards of complexity and sophistication, so simple. There would be no going back. And I could not seem to extricate myself from that black river of emotion that carried me on and on, tugging at me, as if to drown me, and that would not let me go. What else to do but walk the frozen fields as winter began its freezing, white assault, sounding the depths of this river as I walked, searching for its source?

It was then that, despite my efforts to focus on my problem, I found myself thinking about the monk with whom I'd had that breakfast a couple of years earlier. I was remembering, especially, how strange it had been to talk to him—strange and beautiful—because he had managed to defeat the guile that seems to be virtually inborn in all of us. By guile, I mean that wall we put between our true responses and the facade we show the world—varying from that of mere "good manners" to deliberate deceptiveness and attempts to manipulate. It seemed that through solitude, contemplation, chanting, meditating, and through focusing on other things, and at great cost, he had dissolved all his personal guile; he had found his way back to his true self.

I thought, suddenly, *this is what this is about*— "this" being my near-despair, or whatever emotion it was that had reached so deeply into me that I couldn't work, couldn't make sense of anything. It was not just that I had fallen into despair when I discovered the endless guile of even good human beings, even those who had also truly wanted the best for Alex. That was bad enough: the impossibility of ever finding out "the truth" of what had happened to Alex—but that was not the only source of my despair.

I was thinking back to that conversation with the monk mostly because of that surprising thought I'd had when I was talking to him—the one about wanting to be alive. I suppose that I'd meant by that that I had always felt myself to be passively standing on the sidelines, while other people, with what seemed to me to be both utter recklessness and sometimes profound courage, went out and did things and lived. And I had supposed that if they were not necessarily happier for this, or better people, or wiser, they had at least felt—well, I couldn't name what it was, except to say *life* or *Real Life* coursing through their veins. They had known what it is to be a part of it, while I had not.

That is, until I had taken notice of Alex's story, and then, resisting all the way, I backed into telling it, denying even as I did it that I was serious. As resistance to my questioning grew— a nasty interview with an RCMP staff sergeant; a woman screaming in the background as I spoke on the phone to someone else, *Don't talk to her*; a phone tap; the certainty that the police were following me; the strong suspicion that a stranger was listening electronically to one of my interviews, and other scary incidents that I haven't put into this book—perplexed, a bit frightened, filled with both wonder and disgust, I had laid a complaint (specifically about the tapping of my phone) at the door of the director of a high-level body governing police matters in our province.

I thought that he was probably taping our interview—by then I had learned to be wary—and so, at first, I conducted myself with a good bit of guile (even as I knew perfectly well that I wasn't going to be able to keep it up). But our conversation was close to an hour long, and near the end, this tired-looking, undistinguished-appearing, middle-aged man leaned toward me, and even as I left my guile behind (as I had known, with intense exasperation at myself, that I would wind up doing), I saw the intensity now appearing in what had been his mild eyes, how hard he had begun to study me, and I noticed that under the neat striped shirt he was wearing, the sleeves rolled to below his elbow, his shoulders and arms were muscular and strong-looking. If I had conducted myself with guile, not wanting to reveal anything to him, he had clearly done the same, wanting me to think him a harmless, pleasant bureaucrat.

And what had I said to him, when both of us abandoned our guile? I had said, "I won't stop asking questions." I had said, meeting his gaze with my own intensity, "I am a writer. *This* is what writers do."

By struggling to find Alex's story and to tell it, I had entered the stream of life that had always evaded me, that my own fears had kept me from. Alex herself had awakened me, her beautiful promise, her terrible death, her rage at having life snatched from her, her determination that her story would be told. Alex herself had thrust me into life at last. What I had found there had changed me forever. Now it seemed to me that darkness was creeping up, that there was no holding back that black tide of human culpability, human self-interest, human negligence and blindness and self-deception. Of human evil. The real world, it turned out, is almost too terrible to contemplate. All of this was why, after I'd read and absorbed the letter from the daughter of the man who'd been a suspect, I had slowly fallen into that darkness of spirit.

I had wanted only to tell Alex's story, her whole story, accurately, once and for all. Now I saw, too, that that was, and had always been, a hopeless task. The story had grown, year after year, it had rippled out farther and farther from Saskatoon, engaging more and more people, even into the next generation of women—including Angela, whose life had been turned upside down by the news of this long-ago murder—until the beginning and the end and the various middles were hopelessly confused, hopelessly complex, hopelessly compromised. If I felt desperate now, it was because, among other things, I saw at last that there truly is no straight line through this story, a neat beginning, a comprehensible middle, a tidy, satisfying end. I saw that the story was not even the one I had thought it was, not the one I had been trying so hard for so long to tell. The story was, instead, about story.

Somebody, a man, battered, raped, and murdered a beautiful young woman and buried her alive in a shallow grave on the riverbank in Saskatoon, in 1962. Catch the murderer or never catch him, this story of evil keeps on touching people, devastating them. I see now that this story, simply, has no end.

# Acknowledgements

Over the years I asked questions of so many people that it isn't possible to name them all, and I have omitted some people because I doubt they would want to be named, but here is a short list: the Wiwcharuk family, Dave Anderson, Frances Bergles, the staff of CBC Television's *the fifth estate*, Bill Davenport, Laurine Davidson, Anne Davis, Liz Dittmer, Harry Emson, Dennis Fisher, Warren Goulding, Merv Graham, Maureen Grajczyk, Pat Griffiths, Barry Guenther, Norman Haras, Alvin Harms, Tony Harras, Delia Johnston, Cathy Luciuk, Angela McGaffin, Ruth Millar, Holly Mitzel, Merce Montgomery, Gerry Muir, Wilf Popoff, Linda Pylyshyn, Roy Romanow, Candace Savage, Rick Schneider, Anne Smart, William Tesluk, Bill Waiser, Dave Yanko, Zenon Zemluk. I ask the pardon of anyone whose name I have inadvertently omitted. Your contributions are invaluable.

I thank also some retired Saskatoon police officers, some lawyers, and at least one member of the judiciary, who answered my questions about matters of law, or the specific case, or just mused for my benefit on the early sixties in Saskatoon. I thank also directors of the Provincial Board of Police Commissioners and the Office of Public Prosecutions.

I remain in awe of the many librarians who helped me locate facts or who located them for me at the Chinook Regional, Saskatoon, and Regina public libraries, the City of Saskatoon Archives, and the Legislative Library.

As always, my family, my husband, and my son and his family stood by me through thick and thin. I am eternally grateful to them. I am grateful, too, to my agent, Jackie Kaiser, and to Phyllis Bruce at HarperCollins Canada (especially for her patience), and to all of them for their support and assistance.